The Curious Book of Birds

by Abbie Farwell Brown

BOSTON AND NEW YORK HOUGHTON, MIFFLIN AND COMPANY The Riverside Press, Cambridge 1903

There are many books written nowadays which will tell you about birds as folk of the twentieth century see them. They describe carefully the singer's house, his habits, the number of his little wife's eggs, and the color of every tiny feather on her pretty wings. But these books tell you nothing at all about bird-history; about what birds have meant to all the generations of men, women, and children since the world began. You would think, to read the words of the bird-book men, that they were the very first folk to see any bird, and that what they think they have seen is the only matter worth the knowing._

Now the interesting facts about birds we have always with us. We can find them out for ourselves, which is a very pleasant thing to do, or we can take the word of others, of which there is no lack. But it is the quaint fancies about birds which are in danger of being lost. The long-time fancies which the world's children in all lands have been taught are quite as important as the every-day facts. They show what the little feathered brothers have been to the children of men; how we have come to like some and to dislike others as we do; why the poets have called them by certain nicknames which we ought to know; and why a great many strange things are so, in the minds of childlike people._

Facts are not what one looks for in a Curious Book. Yet it may be that some facts have crept in among the ancient fancies of this volume, just as bookworms will crawl into the nicest books; but they do not belong there, and it is for these that the Book apologizes to the children. It has no apology to offer those grown folks who insist that facts, never fancies, are what children need.

CONTENTS

Seven of these tales appeared originally in The Churchman and two in The Congregationalist. They are reprinted by the courteous permission of the publishers of those magazines.

THE DISOBEDIENT WOODPECKER

Long, long ago, at the beginning of things, they say that the Lord made the world smooth and round like an apple. There were no hills nor mountains: nor were there any hollows or valleys to hold the seas and rivers, fountains and pools, which the world of men would need. It must, indeed, have been a stupid and ugly earth in those days, with no chance for swimming or sailing, rowing or fishing. But as yet there was no one to think anything about it, no one who would long to swim, sail, row, and fish. For this was long before men were created.

The Lord looked about Him at the flocks of newly made birds, who were preening their wings and wondering at their own bright feathers, and said to Himself,--

"I will make these pretty creatures useful, from the very beginning, so that in after time men shall love them dearly. Come, my birds," He cried, "come hither to me, and with the beaks which I have given you hollow me out here, and here, and here, basins for the lakes and pools which I intend to fill with water for men and for you, their friends. Come, little brothers, busy yourselves as you would wish to be happy hereafter."

Then there was a twittering and fluttering as the good birds set to work with a will, singing happily over the work which their dear Lord had given them to do. They pecked and they pecked with their sharp little bills; they scratched and they scratched with their sharp little claws, till in the proper places they had hollowed out great basins and valleys and long river beds, and little holes in the ground.

Then the Lord sent great rains upon the earth until the hollows which the birds had made were filled with water, and so became rivers and lakes, little brooks and fountains, just as we see them to-day. Now it was a beautiful, beautiful world, and the good birds sang happily and rejoiced in the work which they had helped, and in the sparkling water which was sweet to their taste.

All were happy except one. The Woodpecker had taken no part with the other busy birds. She was a lazy, disobedient creature, and when she heard the Lord's commands she had only said, "Tut tut!" and sat still on the branch where she had perched, preening her pretty feathers and admiring her silver stockings. "You can toil if you want to," she said to the other birds who wondered at her, "but I shall do no such dirty work. My clothes are too fine."

Now when the world was quite finished and the beautiful water sparkled and glinted here and there, cool and refreshing, the Lord called the birds to Him and thanked them for their help, praising them for their industry and zeal. But to the Woodpecker He said,--

"As for you, O Woodpecker, I observe that your feathers are unruffled by work and that there is no spot of soil upon your beak and claws. How did you manage to keep so neat?"

The Woodpecker looked sulky and stood upon one leg.

"It is a good thing to be neat," said the Lord, "but not if it comes from shirking a duty. It is good to be dainty, but not from laziness. Have you not worked with your brothers as I commanded you?"

"It was such very dirty work," piped the Woodpecker crossly; "I was afraid of spoiling my pretty bright coat and my silver shining hose."

"Oh, vain and lazy bird!" said the Lord sadly. "Have you nothing to do but show off your fine clothes and give yourself airs? You are no more beautiful than many of your brothers, yet they all obeyed me willingly. Look at the snow-white Dove, and the gorgeous Bird of Paradise, and the pretty Grosbeak. They have worked nobly, yet their plumage is not injured. I fear that you must be punished for your disobedience, little Woodpecker. Henceforth you shall wear stockings of sooty black instead of the shining silver ones of which you are so proud. You who were too fine to dig in the earth shall ever be pecking at dusty wood. And as you declined to help in building the water-basins of the world, so you shall never sip from them when you are thirsty. Never shall you thrust beak into lake or river, little rippling brook or cool, sweet fountain. Raindrops falling scantily from the leaves shall be your drink, and your voice shall be heard only when other creatures are hiding themselves from the approaching storm."

It was a sad punishment for the Woodpecker, but she certainly deserved it. Ever since that time, whenever we hear a little tap-tapping in the tree city, we know that it is the poor Woodpecker digging at the dusty wood, as the Lord said she should do. And when we spy her, a dusty little body with black stockings, clinging upright to the tree trunk, we see that she is creeping, climbing, looking up eagerly toward the sky, longing for the rain to fall into her thirsty beak. She is always hoping for the storm to come, and plaintively pipes, "_Plui-plui!_ Rain, O Rain!" until the drops begin to patter on the leaves.

MOTHER MAGPIE'S KINDERGARTEN

Did you ever notice how different are the nests which the birds build in springtime, in tree or bush or sandy bank or hidden in the grass? Some are wonderfully wrought, pretty little homes for birdikins. But others are clumsy, and carelessly fastened to the bough, most unsafe cradles for the feathered baby on the treetop. Sometimes after a heavy wind you find on the ground under the nest poor little broken eggs which rolled out and lost their chance of turning into birds with safe, safe wings of their own. Now such sad things as this happen because in their youth the lazy father and mother birds did not learn their lesson when Mother Magpie had her class in nest-making. The clumsiest nest of all is that which the Wood-Pigeon tries to build. Indeed, it is not a nest at all, only the beginning of one. And there is an old story about this, which I shall tell you.

In the early springtime of the world, when birds were first made, none of them--except Mother Magpie--knew how to build a nest. In that lovely garden where they lived the birds went fluttering about trying their new wings, so interested in this wonderful game of flying that they forgot all about preparing a home for the baby birds who were to come. When the time came to lay their eggs the parents knew not what to do. There was no place safe from the four-legged creatures who cannot fly, and they began to twitter helplessly: "Oh, how I wish I had a nice warm nest for my eggs!" "Oh, what shall we do for a home?" "Dear me! I don't know anything about housekeeping." And the poor silly things ruffled up their feathers and looked miserable as only a little bird can look when it is unhappy.

All except Mother Magpie! She was not the best--oh, no!--but she was the cleverest and wisest of all the birds; it seemed as if she knew everything that a bird could know. Already she had found out a way, and was busily building a famous nest for herself. She was indeed a clever bird! She gathered turf and sticks, and with clay bound them firmly together in a stout elm tree. About her house she built a fence of thorns to keep away the burglar birds who had already begun mischief among their peaceful neighbors. Thus she had a snug and cosy dwelling finished before the others even suspected what she was doing. She popped into her new house and sat there comfortably, peering out through the window-slits with her sharp little eyes. And she saw the other birds hopping about and twittering helplessly.

"What silly birds they are!" she croaked. "Ha, ha! What would they not give for a nest like mine!"

But presently a sharp-eyed Sparrow spied Mother Magpie sitting in her nest.

"Oho! Look there!" he cried. "Mother Magpie has found a way. Let us ask her to teach us."

Then all the other birds chirped eagerly, "Yes, yes! Let us ask her to teach us!"

So, in a great company, they came fluttering, hopping, twittering up to the elm tree where Mother Magpie nestled comfortably in her new house.

"O wise Mother Magpie, dear Mother Magpie," they cried, "teach us how to build our nests like yours, for it is growing night, and we are tired and sleepy."

The Magpie said she would teach them if they would be a patient, diligent, obedient class of little birds. And they all promised that they would.

She made them perch about her in a great circle, some on the lower branches of the trees, some on the bushes, and some on the ground among the grass and flowers. And where each bird perched, there it was to build its nest. Then Mother Magpie found clay and bits of twigs and moss and grass--everything a bird could need to build a nest; and there is scarcely anything you can think of which some bird would not find very useful. When these things were all piled up before her she told every bird to do just as she did. It was like a great big kindergarten of birds playing at a new building game, with Mother Magpie for the teacher.

She began to show them how to weave the bits of things together into nests, as they should be made. And some of the birds, who were attentive and careful, soon saw how it was done, and started nice homes for themselves. You have seen what wonderful swinging baskets the Oriole makes for his baby-cradle? Well, it was the Magpie who taught him how, and he was the prize pupil, to be sure. But some of the birds were not like him, nor like the patient little Wren. Some of them were lazy and stupid and envious of Mother Magpie's cosy nest, which was already finished, while theirs was yet to do.

As Mother Magpie worked, showing them how, it seemed so very simple that they were ashamed not to have discovered it for themselves. So, as she went on bit by bit, the silly things pretended that they had known all about it from the first--which was very unpleasant for their teacher.

Mother Magpie took two sticks in her beak and began like this: "First of all, my friends, you must lay two sticks crosswise for a foundation, thus," and she placed them carefully on the branch before her.

"Oh yes, oh yes!" croaked old Daddy Crow, interrupting her rudely. "I thought that was the way to begin."

Mother Magpie snapped her eyes at him and went on, "Next you must lay a feather on a bit of moss, to start the walls."

"Certainly, of course," screamed the Jackdaw. "I knew that came next. That is what I told the Parrot but a moment since."

Mother Magpie looked at him impatiently, but she did not say anything. "Then, my friends, you must place on your foundation moss, hair, feathers, sticks, and grass--whatever you choose for your house. You must place them like this."

"Yes, yes," cried the Starling, "sticks and grass, every one knows how to do that! Of course, of course! Tell us something new."

Now Mother Magpie was very angry, but she kept on with her lesson in spite of these rude and silly interruptions. She turned toward the Wood-Pigeon, who was a rattle-pated young thing, and who was not having any success with the sticks which she was trying to place.

"Here, Wood-Pigeon," said Mother Magpie, "you must place those sticks through and across, criss-cross, criss-cross, so."

"Criss-cross, criss-cross, so," interrupted the Wood-Pigeon. "I know. That will do-o-o, that will do-o-o!"

Mother Magpie hopped up and down on one leg, so angry she could hardly croak.

"You silly Pigeon," she sputtered, "not so. You are spoiling your nest. Place the sticks so!"

"I know, I know! That will do-o-o, that will do-o-o!" cooed the Wood-Pigeon obstinately in her soft, foolish little voice, without paying the least attention to Mother Magpie's directions.

"We all know that--anything more?" chirped the chorus of birds, trying to conceal how anxious they were to know what came next, for the nests were only half finished.

But Mother Magpie was thoroughly disgusted, and refused to go on with the lesson which had been so rudely interrupted by her pupils.

"You are all so wise, friends," she said, "that surely you do not need any help from me. You say you know all about it,--then go on and finish your nests by yourselves. Much luck may you have!" And away she flew to her own cosy nest in the elm tree, where she was soon fast asleep, forgetting all about the matter.

But oh! What a pickle the other birds were in! The lesson was but half finished, and most of them had not the slightest idea what to do next. That is why to this day many of the birds have never learned to build a perfect nest. Some do better than others, but none build like Mother Magpie.

But the Wood-Pigeon was in the worst case of them all. For she had only the foundation laid criss-cross as the Magpie had shown her. And so, if you find in the woods the most shiftless, silly kind of nest that you can imagine--just a platform of sticks laid flat across a branch, with no railing to keep the eggs from rolling out, no roof to keep the rain from soaking in--when you see that foolishness, you will know that it is the nest of little Mistress Wood-Pigeon, who was too stupid to learn the lesson which Mother Magpie was ready to teach.

And the queerest part of all is that the birds blamed the Magpie for the whole matter, and have never liked her since. But, as you may have found out for yourselves, that is often the fate of wise folk who make discoveries or who do things better than others.

THE GORGEOUS GOLDFINCH

The Goldfinch who lives in Europe is one of the gaudiest of the little feathered brothers. He is a very Joseph of birds in his coat of many colors, and folk often wonder how he came to have feathers so much more gorgeous than his kindred. But after you have read this tale you will wonder no longer.

You must know that when the Father first made all the birds they were dressed alike in plumage of sober gray. But this dull uniform pleased Him no more than it did the birds themselves, who begged that they might wear each the particular style which was most becoming, and by which they could be recognized afar.

So the Father called the birds to Him, one by one, as they stood in line, and dipping His brush in the rainbow color-box painted each appropriately in the colors which it wears to-day. (Except, indeed, that some had later adventures which altered their original hues, as you shall hear in due season.)

But the Goldfinch did not come with the other birds. That tardy little fellow was busy elsewhere on his own affairs and heeded not the Father's command to fall in line and wait his turn for being made beautiful.

So it happened that not until the painting was finished and all the birds had flown away to admire themselves in the water-mirrors of the earth, did the Goldfinch present himself at the Father's feet out of breath.

"O Father!" he panted, "I am late. But I was so busy! Pray forgive me and permit me to have a pretty coat like the others."

"You are late indeed," said the Father reproachfully, "and all the coloring has been done. You should have come when I bade you. Do you not know that it is the prompt bird who fares best? My rainbow color-box has been generously used, and I have but little of each tint left. Yet I will paint you with the colors that I have, and if the result be ill you have only yourself to blame."

The Father smiled gently as He took up the brush which He had laid down, and dipped it in the first color which came to hand. This He used until there was no more, when He began with another shade, and so continued until the Goldfinch was completely colored from head to foot. Such a gorgeous coat! His forehead and throat were of the most brilliant crimson. His cap and sailor collar were black. His back was brown and yellow, his breast white, his wings golden set off with velvet black, and his tail was black with white-tipped feathers. Certainly there was no danger of his being mistaken for any other bird.

When the Goldfinch looked down into a pool and saw the reflection of his gorgeous coat, he burst out into a song of joy. "I like it, oh, I like it!" he warbled, and his song was very sweet. "Oh, I am glad that I was late, indeed I am, dear Father!"

But the kind Father sighed and shook His head as He put away the brush, exclaiming, "Poor little Goldfinch! You are indeed a beautiful bird. But I fear that the gorgeous coat which you wear, and which is the best that I could give you, because you came so late, will cause you more sorrow than joy. Because of it you will be chased and captured and kept in captivity; and your life will be spent in mourning for the days when you were a plain gray bird."

And so it happened. For to this day the Goldfinch is persecuted by human folk who admire his wonderful plumage and his beautiful song. He is kept captive in a cage, while his less gorgeous brothers fly freely in the beautiful world out of doors.

KING OF THE BIRDS

Once upon a time, when the world was very new and when the

birds had just learned from Mother Magpie how to build their nests, some one said, "We ought to have a king. Oh, we need a king of the birds very much!"

For you see, already in the Garden of Birds trouble had begun. There were disputes every morning as to which was the earliest bird who was entitled to the worm. There were quarrels over the best places for nest-building and over the fattest bug or beetle; and there was no one to settle these difficulties. Moreover, the robber birds were growing too bold, and there was no one to rule and punish them. There was no doubt about it; the birds needed a king to keep them in order and peace.

So the whisper went about, "We must have a king. Whom shall we choose for our king?"

They decided to hold a great meeting for the election. And because the especial talent of a bird is for flying, they agreed that the bird who could fly highest up into the blue sky, straight toward the sun, should be their king, king of all the feathered tribes of the air.

Therefore, after breakfast one beautiful morning, the birds met in the garden to choose their king. All the birds were there, from the largest to the smallest, chirping, twittering, singing on every bush and tree and bit of dry grass, till the noise was almost as great as nowadays at an election of two-legged folk without feathers. They swooped down in great clouds, till the sky was black with them, and they were dotted on the grass like punctuation marks on a green page. There were so many that not even wise Mother Magpie or old Master Owl could count them, and they all talked at the same time, like ladies at an afternoon tea, which was very confusing.

Little Robin Redbreast was there, hopping about and saying pleasant things to every one, for he was a great favorite. Gorgeous

Goldfinch was there, in fine feather; and little Blackbird, who was then as white as snow. There were the proud Peacock and the silly Ostrich, the awkward Penguin and the Dodo, whom no man living has ever seen. Likewise there were the Jubjub Bird and the Dinky Bird, and many other curious varieties that one never finds described in the wise Bird Books,--which is very strange, and sad, too, I think. Yes, all the birds were there for the choosing of their king, both the birds who could fly, and those who could not. (But for what were they given wings, if not to fly? How silly an Ostrich must feel!)

Now the Eagle expected to be king. He felt sure that he could fly higher than any one else. He sat apart on a tall pine tree, looking very dignified and noble, as a future king should look. And the birds glanced at one another, nodded their heads, and whispered, "He is sure to be elected king. He can fly straight up toward the sun without winking, and his great wings are so strong, so strong! He never grows tired. He is sure to be king."

Thus they whispered among themselves, and the Eagle heard them, and was pleased. But the little brown Wren heard also, and he was not pleased. The absurd little bird! He wanted to be king himself, although he was one of the tiniest birds there, who could never be a protector to the others, nor stop trouble when it began. No, indeed! Fancy him stepping as a peacemaker between a robber Hawk and a bloody Falcon. It was they who would make pieces of him. But he was a conceited little creature, and saw no reason why he should not make a noble sovereign.

"I am cleverer than the Eagle," he said to himself, "though he is so much bigger. I will be king in spite of him. Ha-ha! We shall see what we shall see!" For the Wren had a great idea in his wee little head-- an idea bigger than the head itself, if you can explain how that could be. He ruffled up his feathers to make himself as huge as possible, and hopped over to the branch where the Eagle was sitting.

"Well, Eagle," said the Wren pompously, "I suppose you expect to be king, eh?"

The Eagle stared hard at him with his great bright eyes. "Well, if I do, what of that?" he said. "Who will dispute me?"

"I shall," said the Wren, bobbing his little brown head and wriggling his tail saucily.

"You!" said the Eagle. "Do you expect to fly higher than I?"

"Yes," chirped the Wren, "I do. Yes, I do, do, do!"

"Ho!" said the Eagle scornfully. "I am big and strong and brave. I can fly higher than the clouds. You, poor little thing, are no bigger than a bean. You will be out of breath before we have gone twice this tree's height."

"Little as I am, I can mount higher than you," said the Wren.

"What will you wager, Wren?" asked the Eagle. "What will you give me if I win?"

"If you win you will be king," said the Wren. "But beside that, if you win I will give you my fat little body to eat for your breakfast. But if I win, Sir, I shall be king, and you must promise never, never, never, to hurt me or any of my people."

"Very well. I promise," said the Eagle haughtily. "Come now, it is time for the trial, you poor little foolish creature."

The birds were flapping their wings and singing eagerly, "Let us begin--begin. We want to see who is to be king. Come, birds, to the trial. Who can fly the highest? Come!"

Then the Eagle spread his great wings and mounted leisurely into the air, straight toward the noonday sun. And after him rose a number of other birds who wanted to be king,--the wicked Hawk, the bold Albatross, and the Skylark singing his wonderful song. The long-legged Stork started also, but that was only for a joke. "Fancy me for a king!" he cried, and he laughed so that he had to come down again in a minute. But the Wren was nowhere to be seen. The truth was, he had hopped ever so lightly upon the Eagle's head, where he sat like a tiny crest. But the Eagle did not know he was there.

Soon the Hawk and the Albatross and even the brave little Skylark fell behind, and the Eagle began to chuckle to himself at his easy victory. "Where are you, poor little Wren?" he cried very loudly, for he fancied that the tiny bird must be left far, far below.

"Here I am, here I am, away up above you, Master Eagle!" piped the Wren in a weak little voice. And the Eagle fancied the Wren was so far up in the air that even his sharp eyes could not spy the tiny creature. "Dear me!" said he to himself. "How extraordinary that he has passed me." So he redoubled his speed and flew on, higher, higher.

Presently he called out again in a tremendous voice, "Well, where are you now? Where are you now, poor little Wren?"

Once more he heard the tiny shrill voice from somewhere above piping, "Here I am, here I am, nearer the sun than you, Master Eagle. Will you give up now?"

Of course the Eagle would not give up yet. He flew on, higher and higher, till the garden and its flock of patient birds waiting for their king grew dim and blurry below. And at last even the mighty wings of the Eagle were weary, for he was far above the clouds. "Surely," he thought, "now the Wren is left miles behind." He gave a scream of triumph and cried, "Where are you now, poor little Wren? Can you hear me at all, down below there?"

But what was his amazement to hear the same little voice above his head shrilling, "Here I am, here I am, Sir Eagle. Look up and see me, look!" And there, sure enough, he was fluttering above the Eagle's head. "And now, since I have mounted so much higher than you, will you agree that I have won?"

"Yes, you have won, little Wren. Let us descend together, for I am weary enough," cried the Eagle, much mortified; and down he swooped, on heavy, discouraged wings.

"Yes, let us descend together," murmured the Wren, once more perching comfortably on the Eagle's head. And so down he rode on this convenient elevator, which was the first one invented in this world.

When the Eagle nearly reached the ground, the other birds set up a cry of greeting.

"Hail, King Eagle!" they sang. "How high you flew! How near the sun! Did he not scorch your Majesty's feathers? Hail, mighty king!" and they made a deafening chorus. But the Eagle stopped them.

"The Wren is your king, not I," he said. "He mounted higher than I did."

"The Wren? Ha-ha! The Wren! We can't believe that The Wren flew higher than you? No, no!" they all shouted. But just then the Eagle lighted on a tree, and from the top of his head hopped the little

Wren, cocking his head and ruffling himself proudly.

"Yes, I mounted higher than he," he cried, "for I was perched on his head all the while, ha-ha! And now, therefore, I am king, small though I be."

Now the Eagle was very angry when he saw the trick that had been played upon him, and he swooped upon the sly Wren to punish him. But the Wren screamed, "Remember, remember your promise never to injure me or mine!" Then the Eagle stopped, for he was a noble bird and never forgot a promise. He folded his wings and turned away in disgust.

"Be king, then, O cheat and trickster!" he said.

"Cheat and trickster!" echoed the other birds. "We will have no such fellow for our king. Cheat and trickster he is, and he shall be punished. You shall be king, brave Eagle, for without your strength he could never have flown so high. It is you whom we want for our protector and lawmaker, not this sly fellow no bigger than a bean."

So the Eagle became their king, after all; and a noble bird he is, as you must understand, or he would never have been chosen to guard our nation's coat of arms. And besides this you may see his picture on many a banner and crest and coin of gold or silver, so famous has he become.

But the Wren was to be punished. And while the birds were trying to decide what should be done with him, they put him in prison in a mouse-hole and set Master Owl to guard the door. Now while the judges were putting their heads together the lazy Owl fell fast asleep, and out of prison stole the little Wren and was far away before any one could catch him. So he was never punished after all, as he richly deserved to be.

The birds were so angry with old Master Owl for his carelessness that he has never since dared to show his face abroad in daytime, but hides away in his hollow tree. And only at night he wanders alone in the woods, sorry and ashamed.

HALCYONE

The story of the first Kingfisher is a sad one, and you need not read it unless for a very little while you wish to feel sorry.

Long, long ago when the world was new, there lived a beautiful princess named Halcyone. She was the daughter of old 甫 lus, King of the Winds, and lived with him on his happy island, where it was his chief business to keep in order the four boisterous brothers, Boreas, the North Wind, Zephyrus, the West Wind, Auster, the South Wind, and Eurus, the East Wind. Sometimes, indeed, 甫 lus had a hard time of it; for the Winds would escape from his control and rush out upon the sea for their terrible games, which were sure to bring death and destruction to the sailors and their ships. Knowing them so well, for she had grown up with these rough playmates, Halcyone came to dread more than anything else the cruelties which they practiced at every opportunity.

One day the Prince Ceyx came to the island of King 甫 lus. He was the son of Hesperus, the Evening Star, and he was the king of the great land of Thessaly. Ceyx and Halcyone grew to love each other dearly, and at last with the consent of good King 甫 lus, but to the wrath of the four Winds, the beautiful princess went away to be the wife of Ceyx and Queen of Thessaly.

For a long time they lived happily in their peaceful kingdom, but finally came a day when Ceyx must take a long voyage on the sea, to visit a temple in a far country. Halcyone could not bear to have him go, for she feared the dangers of the great deep, knowing well the cruelty of the Winds, whom King 甫 lus had such difficulty in keeping within bounds. She knew how the mischievous brothers loved to rush down upon venturesome sailors and blow them into danger, and she knew that they especially hated her husband because he had carried her away from the island where she had watched the Winds at their terrible play. She begged Ceyx not to go, but he said that it was necessary. Then she prayed that if he must go he would take her with him, for she could not bear to remain behind dreading what might happen.

But Ceyx was resolved that Halcyone should not go. The good king longed to take her with him; no more than she could he smile at the thought of separation. But he also feared the sea, not on his own account, but for his dear wife. In spite of her entreaties he remained firm. If all went well he promised to return in two months' time. But Halcyone knew that she should never see him again as now he spoke.

The day of separation came. Standing heart-broken upon the shore, Halcyone watched the vessel sail away into the East, until as a little speck it dropped below the horizon; then sobbing bitterly she returned to the palace.

Now the king and his men had completed but half their journey when a terrible storm arose. The wicked Winds had escaped from the control of good old 甫 lus and were rushing down upon the ocean to punish Ceyx for carrying away the beautiful Halcyone. Fiercely they blew, the lightning flashed, and the sea ran high; and in the midst of the horrible tumult the good ship went to the bottom with all on board. Thus the fears of Halcyone were proved true, and far from his dear wife poor Ceyx perished in the cruel waves.

That very night when the shipwreck occurred, the sad and fearful Halcyone, sleeping lonely at home, knew in a dream the very calamity which had happened. She seemed to see the storm and the shipwreck, and the form of Ceyx appeared, saying a sad farewell to her. As soon as it was light she rose and hastened to the seashore, trembling with a horrible dread. Standing on the very spot whence she had last seen the fated ship, she looked wistfully over the waste of stormy waters. At last she spied a dark something tossing on the waves. The object floated nearer and nearer, until a huge breaker cast before her on the sand the body of her drowned husband.

"O dearest Ceyx!" she cried. "Is it thus that you return to me?" Stretching out her arms toward him, she leaped upon the sea wall as if she would throw herself into the ocean, which advanced and retreated, seething around his body. But a different fate was to be hers. As she leaped forward two strong wings sprouted from her shoulders, and before she knew it she found herself skimming lightly as a bird over the water. From her throat came sounds of sobbing, which changed as she flew into the shrill piping of a bird. Soft feathers now covered her body, and a crest rose above the forehead which had once been so fair. Halcyone was become a Kingfisher, the first Kingfisher who ever flew lamenting above the waters of the world.

The sad bird fluttered through the spray straight to the body that was tossed upon the surf. As her wings touched the wet shoulders, and as her horny beak sought the dumb lips in an attempt to kiss what was once so dear, the body of Ceyx began to receive new life. The limbs stirred, a faint color returned to the cheeks. At the same moment a change like that which had transformed Halcyone began to pass over her husband. He too was becoming a Kingfisher. He too felt the thrill of wings upon his shoulders, wings which were to bear him up and away out of the sea which had been his death. He too was clad in soft plumage with a kingly crest upon his kingly head. With a faint cry, half of sorrow for what had happened, half of joy for the future in which these two loving ones were at least to be together, Ceyx rose from the surf-swept sand where his lifeless limbs had lain and went skimming over the waves beside Halcyone his wife.

So those unhappy mortals became the first kingfishers, happy at last in being reunited. So we see them still, flying up and down over the waters of the world, royal forms with royal crests upon their heads.

They built their nest of the bones of fish, a stout and well-joined basket which floated on the waves as safely as any little boat. And while their children, the baby Halcyons, lay in this rocking cradle, for seven days in the heart of winter, no storms ever troubled the ocean and mariners could set out upon their voyages without fear.

For while his little grandchildren rocked in their basket, the good King 甫 lus, pitying the sorrows of his daughter Halcyone, was always especially careful to chain up in prison those wicked brothers the Winds, so that they could do no mischief of any kind.

And that is why a halcyon time has come to mean a season of peace and safety.

THE FORGETFUL KINGFISHER

In these days the Kingfisher is a sad and solitary bird, caring not to venture far from the water where she finds her food. Up and down the river banks she goes, uttering a peculiar plaintive cry. What is she saying, and why is she so restless? The American Kingfisher is gray, but her cousin of Europe is a bird of brilliant azure with a breast of rusty red. Therefore it must have been the foreign Kingfisher who was forgetful, as you shall hear.

Long, long after the sorrows of Halcyone, the first Kingfisher, were ended, came the great storm which lasted forty days and forty nights, causing the worst flood which the world has ever known. That was a terrible time. When Father Noah hastened to build his ark, inviting the animals and birds to take refuge with him, the Kingfisher herself

was glad to go aboard. For even she, protected by 甫 lus from the

fury of winds and waters, was not safe while there was no place in all the world for her to rest foot and weary wing. So the Kingfisher fluttered in with the other birds and animals, a strange company! And there they lived all together, Noah and his arkful of pets, for many weary days, while the waters raged and the winds howled outside, and all the earth was covered fathoms deep out of sight below the waves.

But after long weeks the storm ceased, and Father Noah opened the little window in the ark and sent forth the Dove to see whether or not there was land visible on which the ark might find rest. Now after he had sent out the Dove, Noah looked about him at the other birds and animals which crowded around him eagerly, for they were growing very restless from their long confinement, and he said, "Which of you is bravest, and will dare follow our friend the Dove out into the watery world? Ah, here is the Kingfisher. Little mother, you at least, reared among the winds and waters, will not be afraid. Take wing, O Kingfisher, and see if the earth be visible. Then return quickly and bring me faithful word of what you find out yonder."

Day was just beginning to dawn when the Kingfisher, who was

then as gray as gray, flew out from the little window of the ark whence the Dove had preceded her. But hardly had she left the safe shelter of Father Noah's floating home, when there came a tremendous whirlwind which blew her about and buffeted her until she was almost beaten into the waves, which rolled endlessly over the face of the whole earth, covering the high hills and the very mountains. The Kingfisher was greatly frightened. She could not go back into the ark, for the little window was closed, and there was no land anywhere on which she could take refuge. Just think for a moment what a dreadful situation it was! There was nothing for her to do but to fly up, straight up, out of reach from the tossing waves and dashing spray.

The Kingfisher was fresh and vigorous, and her wings were strong and powerful, for she had been resting long days in the quiet ark, eating the provisions which Father Noah had thoughtfully prepared for his many guests. So up, up she soared, above the very clouds, on into the blue ether which lies beyond. And lo! as she did so, her sober gray dress became a brilliant blue, the color caught from the azure of those clear heights. Higher and higher she flew, feeling so free and happy after her long captivity, that she quite forgot Father Noah and the errand upon which she had been sent. Up and up she went, higher than the sun, until at last she saw him rising far beneath her, a beautiful ball of fire, more dazzling, more wonderful than she had ever guessed.

"Hola!" she cried, beside herself with joy at the sight. "There is the dear sun, whom I have not seen for many days. And how near, how beautiful he is! I will fly closer still, now that I have come so near. I will observe him in all his splendor, as no other bird, not even the high-flying, sharp-eyed Eagle, has ever seen him."

And with that the foolish Kingfisher turned her course downward, with such mad, headlong speed that she had scarcely time to feel what terrible, increasing heat shot from the sun's rays, until she was so close upon him that it was too late to escape. Oh, but that was a dreadful moment! The feathers on her poor little breast were scorched and set afire, and she seemed in danger not only of spoiling her beautiful new blue dress but of being burned into a wretched little cinder. Horribly frightened at her danger, the Kingfisher turned once more, but this time toward the rolling waters which covered the earth. Down, down she swooped, until with the hiss of burning feathers she splashed into the cold wetness, putting out the fire which threatened to consume her. Once, twice, thrice, she dipped into the grateful coolness, flirting the drops from her blue plumage, now alas! sadly scorched.

When the pain of her burns was somewhat relieved she had time to think what next she should do. She longed for rest, for refuge, for Father Noah's gentle, caressing hand to which she had grown accustomed during those stormy weeks of companionship in the ark. But where was Father Noah? Where was the ark? On all the rolling sea of water there was no movement of life, no sign of any human presence. Then the Kingfisher remembered her errand, and how carelessly she had performed it. She had been bidden to return quickly; but she had wasted many hours--she could not tell how many--in her forgetful flight. And now she was to be punished indeed, if she could not find her master and the ark of refuge.

The poor Kingfisher looked wildly about. She fluttered here and there, backward and forward, over the weary stretch of waves, crying piteously for her master. He did not answer; there was no ark to be found. The sun set and the night came on, but still she sought eagerly from east to west, from north to south, always in vain. She could never find what she had so carelessly lost.

The truth is that during her absence the Dove, who had done her errand faithfully, returned at last with the olive leaf which told of one spot upon the earth's surface at last uncovered by the waves. Then the ark, blown hither and thither by the same storm which had driven the Kingfisher to fly upward into the ether-blue, had drifted far and far to Mount Ararat, where it ran aground. And Father Noah, disembarking with his family and all the assembled animals, had broken up the ark, intending there to build him a house out of the materials from which it was made. But this was many, many leagues from the place where the poor Kingfisher, lonely and frightened, hovered about, crying piteously for her master.

And even when the waters dried away, uncovering the earth in many places, so that the Kingfisher could alight and build herself a nest, she was never happy nor content, but to this day flies up and down the water-ways of the world piping sadly, looking eagerly for her dear master and for some traces of the ark which sheltered her. And the reflection which she makes in the water below shows an azure-blue body, like a reflection of the sky above, with some of the breast-feathers scorched to a rusty red. And now you know how it all came about.

THE WREN WHO BROUGHT FIRE

Centuries and centuries ago, when men were first made, there was no such thing as fire known in all the world. Folk had no fire with which to cook their food, and so they were obliged to eat it raw; which was very unpleasant, as you may imagine! There were no cheery fireplaces about which to sit and tell stories, or make candy or pop corn. There was no light in the darkness at night except the sun and moon and stars. There were not even candles in those days, to say nothing of gas lamps or electric lights. It is strange to think of such a world where even the grown folks, like the children and the birds, had to go to bed at dusk, because there was nothing else to do.

But the little birds, who lived nearer heaven than men, knew of the fire in the sun, and knew also what a fine thing it would be for the tribes without feathers if they could have some of the magic element.

One day the birds held a solemn meeting, when it was decided that men must have fire. Then some one must fly up to the sun and bring a firebrand thence. Who would undertake this dangerous errand? Already by sad experience the Kingfisher had felt the force of the sun's heat, while the Eagle and the Wren, in the famous flight which they had taken together, had learned the same thing. The assembly of birds looked at one another, and there was a silence.

"I dare not go," said the Kingfisher, trembling at the idea; "I have been up there once, and the warning I received was enough to last me for some time."

"I cannot go," said the Peacock, "for my plumage is too precious to risk."

"I ought not to go," said the Lark, "for the heat might injure my pretty voice."

"I must not go," said the Stork, "for I have promised to bring a baby to the King's palace this evening."

"I cannot go," said the Dove, "for I have a nestful of little ones who depend upon me for food."

"Nor I," said the Sparrow, "for I am afraid." "Nor I!" "Nor I!" "Nor I!" echoed the other birds.

"I will not go," croaked the Owl, "for I simply do not wish to."

Then up spoke the little Wren, who had been keeping in the background of late, because he was despised for his attempt to deceive the birds into electing him their king.

"I will go," said the Wren. "I will go and bring fire to men. I am of little use here. No one loves me. Every one despises me because of the trick which I played the Eagle, our King. No one will care if I am injured in the attempt. I will go and try."

"Bravely spoken, little friend," said the Eagle kindly. "I myself would go but that I am the King, and kings must not risk the lives upon which hangs the welfare of their people. Go you, little Wren, and if you are successful you will win back the respect of your brothers which you have forfeited."

The brave little bird set out upon his errand without further words. And weak and delicate though he was, he flew and he flew up and up so sturdily that at last he reached the sun, whence he plucked a firebrand and bore it swiftly in his beak back toward the earth. Like a falling star the bright speck flashed through the air, drawing ever nearer and nearer to the cool waters of Birdland and the safety which awaited him there. The other birds gathered in a flock about their king and anxiously watched the Wren's approach.

Suddenly the Robin cried out, "Alas! He burns! He has caught fire!" And off darted the faithful little friend to help the Wren. Sure enough, a spark from the blazing brand had fallen upon the plumage of the Wren, and his poor little wings were burning as he fluttered piteously down, still holding the fire in his beak.

The Robin flew up to him and said, "Well done, brother! You have succeeded. Now give me the fire and I will relieve you while you drop into the lake below us to quench the flame which threatens your life."

So the Robin in his turn seized the firebrand in his beak and started down with it. But, like the Wren, he too was soon fluttering in the blaze of his own burning plumage, a little living firework, falling toward the earth.

Then up came the Lark, who had been watching the two unselfish birds. "Give me the brand, brother Robin," she cried, "for your pretty feathers are all ablaze and your life is in danger."

So it was the Lark who finally brought the fire safely to the earth and gave it to mankind. But the Robin and the Wren, when they had put out the flame which burned their feathers, appeared in the assembly of the birds, and were greeted with great applause as the heroes of the day. The Robin's breast was scorched a brilliant red, but the poor, brave little Wren was wholly bare of plumage. All his pretty feathers had been burned away, and he stood before them shivering and piteous.

"Bravo! little Wren," cried King Eagle. "A noble deed you have done this day, and nobly have you won back the respect of your brother birds and earned the everlasting gratitude of men. Now what shall we do to help you in your sorry plight?" After a moment's thought he turned to the other birds and said, "Who will give a feather to help patch a covering for our brave friend?"

"I!" and "I!" and "I!" and "I!" chorused the generous birds. And in turn each came forward with a plume or a bit of down from his breast. The Robin first, who had shared his peril, brought a feather sadly scorched, but precious; the Lark next, who had helped in the time of need. The Eagle bestowed a kingly feather, the Thrush, the Nightingale,--every bird contributed except the Owl.

But the selfish Owl said, "I see no reason why I should give a feather. Hoot! No! The Wren brought me into trouble once, and I will not help him now. Let him go bare, for all my aid."

"Shame! Shame!" cried the birds indignantly. "Old Master Owl, you ought to be ashamed. But if you are so selfish we will not have you in our society. Go back to your hollow tree!"

"Yes, go back to your hollow tree," cried the Eagle sternly; "and when winter comes may you shiver with cold as you would have left the brave little Wren to shiver this day. You shall ruffle your feathers as much as you like, but you will always feel cold at heart, because your heart is selfish."

And indeed, since that day for all his feathers the Owl has never been able to keep warm enough in his lonely hollow tree.

But the Wren became one of the happiest of all the birds, and a favorite both with his feathered brothers and with men, because of his brave deed, and because of the great fire-gift which he had brought from the sun.

HOW THE BLUEBIRD CROSSED

Of course every one knows that the Bluebird was made from a piece of the azure sky itself. One has only to match his wonderful color against the April heaven to be sure of that. Therefore the little Bluebird was especially dear to the Spirit of the sky, the Father in Heaven.

One day this venturesome little bird started out upon a long journey across the wide Pacific Ocean toward this New World which neither Columbus nor any other man had yet discovered. Under him tossed the wide, wide sea, rolling for miles in every direction, with no land visible anywhere on which a little bird might rest his foot. For this was also before there were any islands in all that stretch of waters. Soon the poor little Bluebird became very weary and wished he had not ventured upon so long a flight. His wings began to droop and he sank lower and lower toward the sea which seemed eager to overwhelm his blueness with its own. He had come so far over the salty wastes that he was very thirsty; but with water, water everywhere there was not a drop to drink. The poor little bird glanced despairingly up toward the blue sky from which he had been made and cried,--

"O Spirit of the blue sky, O my Father in Heaven, help your child the Bluebird! Give me, I pray you, a place to rest and refreshment for my thirsty throat, or I perish in the cruel blue waters!"

At these sorrowful words the kind Father took pity upon his little Bluebird. And what do you think? He made a baby earthquake which heaved a rocky point of land up through the waves, just big enough for a little bird's perch. It was a tiny reef, and a crack in the rock held but a few drops of the rain which began to fall; but it meant at least a moment's safety and draught of life for the weary bird, and glad enough he was to reach it.

He had not been there long, however, when a big wave almost washed him away. He was not yet safe. Still he lacked the rest and refreshment which he so sorely needed. For the raindrops were soon turned brackish by the waves which dashed upon the reef from all sides, and the Bluebird had to keep hopping up and down to avoid being drowned in the tossing spray. He was more tired than ever, and this continuous exercise made him even more thirsty. Once more he prayed to the Father for help. And once more the kind Spirit of the Sky heard him from the blueness.

This time there was a terrible earthquake, until the sea boiled and rolled into huge waves as if churned by a mighty churn at the very bottom of things, and with a terrified scream the Bluebird flew high into the air.

But when the noise and the rumbling died away and once more the sea lay calm and still, what do you think the Bluebird saw? The great ocean which had once stretched an unbroken sheet of blue as far as the eye could see was now dotted here and there by islands, big islands and little islands, groups and archipelagoes of them, just as on the map one sees them to-day peppering the Pacific Ocean. Samoa came up, and Tonga, and Tulima, and many others with names quite as bad, if not worse. From one island to another the Bluebird flew, finding rest and refreshment on each, until he reached the mainland in safety. And there the islands remain to this day for other travelers to visit, breaking their journey from west to east or from east to west. There are forests and cascades, springs of fresh and pleasant water, delicious fruits, wonderful birds and animals, and finally a race of strange, dark men. (But they came long, long after.)

So the Bluebird crossed the Pacific, folk tell. Was it not wonderful how the kind Father came to scatter those many islands in the Pacific Ocean,--stepping-stones for a tiny little Bluebird so that he need not wet his feet in crossing that wide salty river?

THE PEACOCK'S COUSIN

Long, long ago in the days of wise King Solomon, the Crow and the Pheasant were the best of friends, and were always seen going about together, wing in wing. Now the Pheasant was the Peacock's own cousin,--a great honor, many thought, for the Peacock was the most gorgeous of all the birds. But it was not altogether pleasant for the Pheasant, because at that time he wore such plain and shabby old garments that his proud relative was ashamed of him, and did not like to be reminded that they were of the same family. When the Peacock went strutting about with his wonderful tail spread fan-wise, and with his vain little eyes peering to see who might be admiring his beauty, the Peacock's cousin and his friend the Crow, who was then a plain white bird, would slink aside and hide behind a tree, whence they would peep enviously until the Peacock had passed by. Then the Peacock's cousin would say,--

"Oh, how beautiful, how grand, how noble he is! How came such a lordly bird to have for a cousin so homely a creature as I?"

But the Crow would answer, trying to comfort his friend, "Yes, he is gorgeous. But listen, what a harsh and disagreeable voice he has! And see how vain he is. I would not be so vain had I so scandalous a tale in my family history."

Then the Crow told the Peacock's cousin how his proud relative came to have so unmusical a voice.

* * * * *

When Adam and Eve were living peacefully in their fair garden, while Satan was still seeking in vain a way to enter there, the Peacock was the most beautiful of all the companions who surrounded the happy pair. His plumage shone like pearl and emerald, and his voice was so melodious that he was selected to sing the Lord's praises every day in the streets of heaven. But he was then, as now, very, very vain; and Satan, prowling about outside the wall of Paradise, saw this.

"Aha!" he said to himself, "here is the vainest creature in all the world. He is the one I must flatter in order to win entrance to the garden, where I am to work my mischief. Let me approach the Peacock."

Satan stole softly to the gate and in a wheedling voice called to the Peacock,--

"O most wonderful and beautiful bird! Are you one of the birds of Paradise?"

"Yes, I am one of the dwellers in the happy garden," answered the Peacock, strutting. "But who are you who slink about so secretly, as if afraid of some one?"

"I am one of the cherubim who are appointed to sing the Lord's praises," answered the wicked Satan. "I have stopped for a moment to visit the Paradise which He has prepared for the blest, and I find as my first glimpse of its glories you, O most lovely bird! Will you conceal me under your rainbow wings and bring me within the walls?"

"I dare not," answered the Peacock. "The Lord allows none to enter here. He will be angry and will punish me."

"O charming bird!" went on Satan with his smooth tongue, "take me with you, and I will teach you three mysterious words which shall preserve you forever from sickness, age, and death."

At this promise the Peacock was greatly tempted and began to hesitate in his refusals. And at last he said,--

"I dare not myself let you in, O stranger, but if you keep your promise I will send the Serpent, who is wiser than I and who may more easily find some way to let you enter unobserved."

So it was through the Peacock that Satan met the vile Serpent, whose shape he assumed in order to enter the garden and tempt Eve with the apple. And for the Peacock's share in the doings of that dreadful day the Lord took away his beautiful voice and sent him forth from the pleasant garden to chatter harshly in this workaday world, where his gorgeousness and his vanity are but a reminder to men of the shame which he brought upon their ancestors.

* * * * *

"And therefore," said the Crow, concluding his gossip, "therefore, dear Pheasant, I see no reason why we should envy your cousin. We are very plain citizens of Birdland, but we are at least respectable. I like you much better, having nothing to make you vain, nothing of which to be ashamed."

* * * * *

So the Crow spoke, in the wisdom which he had learned from Solomon. But the Peacock's cousin refused to be comforted. The shabbiness of his coat preyed upon his mind, and he fancied that the other birds jeered at him because in such old clothes he dared to be the Peacock's cousin. It seemed to him that every day the Peacock himself grew more haughty and more patronizing.

One day the Crow and the Peacock's cousin were sauntering through the Malay woods when they met the Peacock face to face. The Crow looked defiant and stood jauntily; but the Pheasant tried to shrink out of sight. The Peacock, however, had spied his poor relative, and was filled with cousinly resentment at his appearance.

He stopped short. He stood upon one leg. He puffed and ruffled himself, spreading out his thousand-eyed tail so that its colors flashed wonderfully in the sunshine. He frilled his neck feathers and snapped his mean little eyes maliciously; then turning his back on the shabby couple said, as he stepped airily away,--

"Ah, I have dropped some of my old feathers back there a little way. You can have them if you like, Pheasant. They will freshen you up a bit; you really are looking shockingly seedy. But for mercy's sake don't wear them in my presence! I can't bear to see any one parading in my cast-off elegance." Then the Peacock minced away.

The Peacock's cousin stamped on the ground and flapped his wings with rage. If he had been a girl he would have burst into tears. "I cannot stand this," he cried. "To be treated as if I were a beggar! To be given old clothes to wear! Crow, Crow, if you were any kind of friend you would help me. But you stand staring there and see me insulted, without turning a feather! What is the use of all your wisdom that you learned from King Solomon if you cannot help a friend in need? I tell you, I must have some better garments, or I shall die of mortification."

"Don't be excited," said the Crow soothingly. "I have been thinking the matter over, and I believe I can do something. Listen. Yesterday I found brushes and a box of colors in a room of the King's palace. They belonged to the Court Painter. Now they belong to me, for I have hidden them away in a hollow tree where no one else can find them. I thought they might be useful, and I think so still."

"Well, well! What do you propose to do with paints and brushes?" cried the Peacock's cousin impatiently.

"I propose to paint you, to varnish you, to gild you," patiently answered the Crow.

"Oh, you dear Crow!" exclaimed the other, clapping his wings. "You will make me brilliant and beautiful! You will make me worthy of the Peacock, will you not? How clever of you to think of such a thing!"

"Yes," replied the Crow; "I watched the Court Painter at work in the garden one day, and I know how it is done. I will make you as gorgeous as you wish. But you must return the compliment. If you are to be an ornament of fashion, so must I be; for are we not inseparable cronies? And when you become beautiful it would not do for you to be seen with such a dowdy as I am."

"You dear creature!" said the Peacock's cousin affectionately; "of course we will share alike. I will paint you as soon as I see how you succeed with me. Ah, I know your skill in everything. You will be a fine artist, my friend! But come, let us get to work at once."

So the flattered Crow led him to the hollow tree where he had concealed the brushes and the gilding and the India ink, and all the gorgeous changeable tints which an Eastern artist uses in his paintings. "Here we are," said the Crow. "Now let us see what we shall see, when Master Crow turns painter."

The Crow set to work with a will, splashing on the colors generously, gold and green and bronze iridescence. He had the Peacock in mind, and though he did not exactly copy the plumage of that wonderful bird, he managed to suggest the cousinship of the Pheasant in the golden eyes of his long and beautiful tail. When he had finished, the Crow was delighted with his work.

"Ah!" he cried. "Now bend over this fountain, my dear friend, and observe yourself. I think you do credit to my skill as an artist, eh?"

The Peacock's cousin hurried down to the water-pool, all in a flutter of excitement. And when he saw his image he cried, "How beautiful, how truly beautiful, I am! Why, I am quite as handsome as Peacock himself. Surely, now he need not be ashamed to call me cousin. I shall move in the most fashionable circles. Heavens! Look at my lovely tail! Look at my burnished feathers! I must go immediately and show my new dress to Cousin Peacock. I should not be surprised if he became jealous of my gorgeousness." And off he started as fast as he could go.

"Hold on!" cried the Crow. "Don't run away so quickly. You have forgotten something. Don't you remember that you promised to paint me beautiful like yourself?"

"Oh, bother!" answered the ungrateful friend, tossing his head. "I have no time now for such business. I must hasten to my cousin, for this is a matter of family pride. Run along like a good creature; and by the way, you may as well gather the feathers which Peacock mentioned. I am sure they will make you look quite respectable. Besides, I will give you some of mine when I have worn them a little. Ta-ta!" And he stepped airily away.

But the Crow strode after him, shaking his wings and crying, "Come back, come back and perform your part of the bargain, you selfish, ungrateful creature!" And he caught the Pheasant by one of his long tail-feathers.

"Let go my train, impertinent wretch!" shrieked the Peacock's cousin, turning upon him fiercely. "I tell you I have no time to spend in such nonsense. I must be presenting myself in high society."

"Villain!" croaked the Crow, and he rushed forward fiercely, intending to tear out the beautiful feathers which he had painted for his ungrateful friend. Thereupon the Pheasant exclaimed,--

"You want to be painted, do you? Well, take that!" and, seizing the bottle of India ink which was in the Eastern artist's paint-box, he hurled it at the poor Crow, deluging with blackness his spotless feathers. Then laughing harshly, away he flew to his cousin the Peacock, who received him with proud affection, because they were now really birds of a feather. For the Peacock's cousin was become one of the most beautiful birds in the world.

But the poor Crow was now a sombre, black bird, wearing the seedy-looking, inky coat which we know so well to-day. His heart was broken by his friend's faithlessness, and he became a sour cynic who can see no good in anything. He flies about crying "Caw! Caw!" in the most disagreeable, sarcastic tone, as if sneering at the mean action of that Malay bird, which he can never forget.

THE MASQUERADING CROW

The Crow became very sour and disagreeable after his friend the Peacock's cousin deserted him for more gorgeous company. Though he pretended not to care because the Pheasant was now a proud, beautifully-coated dandy, while he was the shabbiest of all the birds in his coat of rusty black, yet in truth he did care very much. He could not forget how the Peacock's cousin had dyed him this sombre hue, after promising to paint him bright and wonderful, like himself. He could not help thinking how fine he would have looked in similar plumage of a rainbow tint, or how becoming a long swallow-tail would be to his style of beauty. He wished that there was a tailor in Birdland to whom he could go for a new suit of clothes. But alas! There seemed no way but for him to remain ugly old Crow to the end of the chapter.

The Crow went moping about most unhappily while this was preying on his mind, until he really became somewhat crazy upon the subject. The only thing about which he could think was clothes--clothes--clothes; and that is indeed a foolish matter to absorb one's mind. One word of the Peacock's cousin remained in his memory and refused to be forgotten. He had advised the Crow to gather up the feathers which had fallen from the Peacock's plumage and to make himself fine with them. First the Crow remembered these words sadly, because they showed the unkind heart of his old friend. Next he remembered them with scorn, because they showed vanity.

Then he remembered them with interest because they gave him an idea. And that idea gradually grew bigger and bigger until it became a plan.

The plan came to him completely one day while he was sitting moodily on a tree watching the Peacock and his cousin sweeping proudly over the velvet lawn of the King's garden. For nowadays the Pheasant moved in the most courtly circles, as he had promised himself. As they passed under the Crow two beautiful feathers fell behind them and lay on the grass shining in the sunlight with a hundred colors.

"Once more the cast-off plumage of the Peacock family is left for me!" croaked the Crow to himself. "Am I only to be made beautiful by borrowing from others? Perhaps I might collect feathers enough from all the birds to conceal my inky coat. Aha! I have it." And this was the plan of the Crow. He would steal from every dweller in Birdland a feather, and see whether he could not make himself more beautiful than the Peacock's cousin himself.

Now the Crow was a skilful thief. He could steal the silver off the King's table from under the steward's very nose. He could steal a maid's thimble from her finger as she nodded sleepily over her work. He could steal the pen from behind a scribe's ear, as he paused to scratch his head and think over the spelling of a word. So the Crow felt sure that he could steal their feathers from the birds without any trouble.

When the Peacock and his cousin had passed by, the Crow swooped down and carried off the two feathers which were to begin his collection. He hid them in his treasure-house in the hollow tree, and started out for more.

It was great fun for the Crow, and he almost forgot to be miserable.

He followed old lady Ostrich about for some time before he dared tweak a handful of feathers from her tail. But finally he succeeded; and though she squawked horribly and turned, quick as a flash, she was not quick enough to catch the nimble thief, who was already hidden under a bush. In the same way he secured some lovely plumes from the Bird of Paradise, the Parrot, and the Cock. He robbed the Redbreast of his ruddy vest, the Hoopoe of his crown, and he secured a swallow-tail which he had long coveted. He took some rosy-redness from the Flamingo, the gilding of the Goldfinch, the gray down of an Eider-Duck. He burgled the Bluebird and the Redbird and the Yellowbird; and not one single feathered creature escaped his clever beak. At last his hole in the tree was brimming with feathers of every color, length, and degree of softness, a gorgeous feather-bed on which it would dazzle one to sleep.

Then the Crow set to work to make himself a coat of many colors, like Joseph's. He was a very clever bird, and a wondrous coat it turned out to be. It had no particular cut nor style; it was not like the coat which any bird had ever before worn. The feathers were placed in any fashion that happened to please his original fancy. Some pointed up and some down; some were straight and some were curled; some drooped about his feet and others curved gracefully over his head; some trailed far behind. He was completely covered from top to toe, so that not one blot of his own inky feathers showed through the gorgeousness. A red vest he wore, and a swallow-tail, of course, and there was a crown of feathers on his head. Never was there seen a more extraordinary bird nor one more gaudy. Perhaps he was not in the best of taste, but at least he was striking.

When all was finished the Crow went and looked at himself in the fountain mirror; and he was much pleased.

"Well now!" he cried. "How am I for a bird? I believe no one will know me, and that is just as well; for now I am so fine that I shall myself refuse to know any one. Ho! This ought to give some ideas to that conceited Peacock family! I am a self-made man. I am an artist who knows how to adapt his materials. I am a genius. King Solomon himself will wonder at my glory. And as for the Eagle, King of the Birds, he will grow pale with envy. King of the Birds, indeed! It is now I who should rightfully be King. No other ever wore clothes so fine as mine. By right of them I ought to be King of the Birds. I will be King of the Birds!"

You see the poor old Crow was quite crazy with his one idea.

Forth he stalked into Birdland to show his gorgeous plumage and to get himself elected King of the Birds. The first persons he met were the Peacock and his cousin,--he who was once the Crow's best friend. The Crow ruffled himself his prettiest when he saw them coming.

"Good gracious! Who is that extraordinary fowl?" drawled the Peacock. "He must be some great noble from a far country."

"How beautiful!" murmured his silly cousin. "How odd! How fascinating! How distinguished! I wish the Crow had painted me like that!" The Crow heard these words and swelled with pride, casting a scornful glance at his old friend as he swept by.

Next he met a little Sparrow who was picking bugs from the grass. "Out of my way, Birdling!" cried the Crow haughtily. "I am the King."

"The King!" gasped the Sparrow, nearly choking over a fat bug, he was so surprised. "I did not know that the King wore such a robe. How gorgeous--but how queer!"

Next the Crow met Mr. Stork, standing gravely on one leg and thinking of the little baby which he was going to bring that night to the cottage by the lake. The Stork looked up in surprise as the wonderful stranger approached.

"Bless me!" he exclaimed, "whom have we here? I thought I knew all Birdland, but I never before saw such a freak as this!"

[Illustration: _"Bless me!" he exclaimed, "whom have we here?"_]

"I am the King. I am to be the new King," announced the Crow. "Is there any bird more gorgeous than I?"

"Truly, I hope not," said the Stork gravely. "Yet the Woodcock is a very foolish bird. One never knows what he will do next. If he should try to be fashionable"--

But the Crow had passed on without listening to the Stork's sarcasm.

As he went through Birdland he drew behind him a following of feathered citizens, chattering, screaming, tittering all together like the crowd after a circus procession. All the birds, big and little, plain and pretty, flocked to see this wonderful stranger who because of his fine clothes was coming to have himself named King. Some of them thought him truly beautiful, some thought him ridiculous; some envied him, some jeered. But they all stared; and the more they stared the more conceited became the Crow, the more sure that the kingdom was to be his.

At last they came into the presence of the Eagle himself. That royal bird was perched upon his eyrie far up on the cliff. Below him gathered the dense flock of birds, waiting to see what would happen when the Crow demanded to be made King in the Eagle's place. The Eagle had been warned of the matter by the little Humming-Bird, and was looking very majestic and scornful. But the Swallow flew round and round in great circles, twittering excitedly, and in each circle sweeping nearer and nearer to the ground. The Swallow was angry because some one had stolen his beautiful swallow-tail.

Presently the Crow swaggered forth, and cocking his impertinent eye towards the Eagle he croaked,--

"Hello there, Old High-perch! Give me your crown and sceptre, for I am King of the Birds, not you. Look at my gorgeous clothes; look at your own dull plumage. Am I not kingly?--look at me."

The King made no reply, merely gazing sternly at the Crow. But the Swallow took up the word.

"Look at him, look at him indeed, O King!" he screamed. "There is something strange about his kingly plumage. That swallow-tail is mine, I know it!" And with a vicious tweak the Swallow pulled out the long forked feathers of which the Crow was especially proud. Oh, what a shriek of rage the mad old bird gave! At that moment the Hoopoe came up and said, "Ha! Methinks I too recognize my property. This is my crown," and forthwith he snatched the plumes from the Crow's forehead, leaving it quite ugly and bare. Next the gentle Redbreast claimed his vest, and the Bluebird her azure feathers, and the Ostrich her train which she had sorely missed. Each of the birds in turn came up and with much chattering and scolding twitched away the property of which he or she had been robbed, until the Crow stood before them in his customary suit of solemn black, a bird ashamed and sore. For they had pecked him with their bills and beaten him with their wings and scratched him with their claws until even his own plain old coat was frayed and rent.

"Oh ho, oh ho! It is only old Daddy Crow, after all!" screamed the birds in chorus. And then, because the Eagle burst out laughing, they saw that it was really funny. Since the King did not mind being robbed for a time of his title, surely they need not mourn over the few feathers which the thief had borrowed, especially since each now had his own. Chattering with glee they all flew home to their various nests, leaving the Crow alone with his shame and soreness.

Just at this moment the Peacock and his cousin came hurrying up out of breath.

"Oh, what is it? What is the matter? What was all that noise just now?" asked the Peacock.

"Oh, what has become of the beautiful, noble, splendid, remarkable, graceful, gorgeous, stylish, long-tailed, kingly stranger?" questioned the Peacock's cousin, speaking affably to the Crow, for the first time since his adoption into high society.

The Crow looked at him sideways, and all his madness went away as he saw how very, very silly this creature was.

"He was a fool in fools' feathers," he croaked. "He is no more. But before the end he bade me return these to you, saying, 'Fine feathers do not make fine birds.'" Speaking thus, he presented to the pair their two long feathers with which he had started his collection and which were the only ones now remaining to the masquerading Crow.

Then with a harsh Caw! he flew away to his tree. He is not a happy bird, but since that time he has never been so mad as to think that clothes are the chief thing in the world.

KING SOLOMON AND THE BIRDS

King Solomon was wiser than all men, and his fame was in all nations round about Jerusalem. He was so wise that he knew every spoken language; yes, but more than this, he could talk with everything that lived, trees and flowers, beasts and fowls, creeping things and fishes. What a very pleasant thing that was for Solomon, to be sure! And how glad one would be nowadays to have such knowledge!

Solomon was especially fond of birds, and loved to talk with them because their voices were so sweet and they spoke such beautiful words. One day the wise King was chatting pleasantly with the birds who lived in his wonderful garden, and these are some of the things which he heard them say. The Nightingale, the sweetest singer of all, chanted,--

"Contentment is the greatest happiness."

"It would be better for most people never to have been born," crooned the melancholy Turtle-Dove.

The happy little Swallow gave her opinion,--"Do good and you will be rewarded hereafter."

The harsh cry of the Peacock meant, "As thou judgest so shalt thou be judged."

The Hoopoe said, "He who has no pity for others will find none for himself."

The cynical old Crow croaked disagreeably, "The further away from men I am, the better I am pleased."

Last of all the Cock who sings in the morning chanted his joyous song,--"Think of your Creator, O foolish creatures!"

When they had finished talking King Solomon softly stroked the head of the pretty little Dove and bade her cheer up, for life was not so dreadful a thing, after all. And he gave her permission to build her nest under the walls of the great Temple which he was building, the most beautiful, golden house in the whole world. Some years afterward the Doves had so increased in numbers that with their extended wings they formed a veil over the numberless pilgrims who came to Jerusalem to visit the wonderful Temple.

But of all the winged singers who spoke that day in the garden, the wise King chose to have ever near him the Cock, because he had spoken words of piety, and the nimble Hoopoe, because he was able to plunge his clear gaze into the depths of the earth as if it were made of transparent glass and discover the places where springs of living water were hidden under the soil. It was very convenient for Solomon, when he was traveling, to have some one with him who was able to find water in whatsoever place he might be resting.

Thus the Cock and the Hoopoe became Solomon's closest companions; but of the two the Hoopoe was his favorite. The Hoopoe is an Eastern bird and we do not see him in America. He is about as big as a Jay, colored a beautiful reddish gray, with feathers of purple, brown, and white, and his black wings are banded with white. But the peculiar thing about a Hoopoe is his crown of tawny feathers, a tall crown for so small a bird. And this is the story of the Hoopoe's crown.

* * * * *

One day when Solomon was journeying across the desert, he was sorely distressed by the heat of the sun, until he came near to fainting. Just then he spied a flock of his friends the Hoopoes flying past, and calling to them feebly he begged them to shelter him from the burning rays.

The King of the Hoopoes gathered together his whole nation and caused them to fly in a thick cloud over the head of Solomon while he continued his journey. In gratitude the wise King offered to give his feathered friends whatever reward they might ask.

For a whole day the Hoopoes talked the matter over among themselves, then their King came to Solomon and said to him,--

"We have considered your offer, O generous King, and we have decided that what we most desire is to have, each of us, a golden crown on his head."

King Solomon smiled and answered, "Crowns of gold shall you have. But you are foolish birds, my Hoopoes; and when the evil days shall come upon you and you see the folly of your desire, return here to me and I will help you yet again."

So the King of the Hoopoes left King Solomon with a beautiful golden crown upon his head. And soon all the Hoopoes were wearing golden crowns. Thereupon they grew very proud and haughty. They went down by the lakes and pools and strutted there that they might admire themselves in the water mirrors. And the Queen of the Hoopoes became very airy, and refused to speak to her own cousin and to the other birds who had once been her friends.

There was a certain fowler who used to set traps for birds. He put a piece of broken mirror into his trap, and a Hoopoe spying it went in to admire herself, and was caught. The fowler looked at the shining crown upon her head and said, "What have we here! I never saw a crown like this upon any bird. I must ask about this."

So he took the crown to Issachar, the worker in metal, and asked him what it was. Issachar examined it carefully, and his eyes stuck out of his head. But he said carelessly, "It is a crown of brass, my friend. I will give you a quarter of a shekel for it; and if you find any more bring them to me. But be sure to tell no other man of the matter." (A shekel was about sixty-two cents.)

After this the fowler caught many Hoopoes in the same way, and sold their crowns to Issachar. But one day as he was on his way to the metalworker's shop he met a jeweler, and to him he showed one of the Hoopoes' crowns.

"What is this, and where did you find it?" exclaimed the jeweler. "It is pure gold. I will give you a golden talent for every four you bring me." (A talent was worth three hundred shekels.)

Now when the value of the Hoopoes' crowns was known, every one turned fowler and began to hunt the precious birds. In all the land of Israel was heard the twang of bows and the whirling of slings. Bird lime was made in every town, and the price of traps rose in the market so that the trap-makers became rich men. Not a Hoopoe could show his unlucky head without being slain or taken captive, and the days of the Hoopoes were numbered. It seemed that soon there would be no more Hoopoes left to bewail their sad fate.

At last the few who still lived gathered together and held a meeting to consider what should be done, for their minds were filled with sorrow and dismay. And they decided to appeal once more to King Solomon, who had granted their foolish prayer.

Flying by stealth through the loneliest ways, the unhappy King of the Hoopoes came at last to the court of the King, and stood once more before the steps of his golden throne. With tears and groans he related the sad fortune which had befallen his golden-crowned race.

King Solomon looked kindly upon the King of the Hoopoes and said, "Behold, did I not warn you of your folly in desiring to have crowns of gold? Vanity and pride have been your ruin. But now, that there may be a memorial of the service which once you did me, your crowns of gold shall be changed into crowns of feathers, and with them you may walk unharmed upon the earth."

In this way the remaining Hoopoes were saved. For when the fowlers saw that they no longer wore crowns of gold upon their heads, they ceased to hunt them as they had been doing. And from that time forth the family of the Hoopoes have flourished and increased in peace, even to the present day.

* * * * *

Solomon was ever seeking to grow even wiser. The better to know the wonders of God's world and the ways of all creatures, he undertook many journeys,--not as we ordinary poor mortals travel, in heavy wagons or clumsy boats, by dusty roads or stormy waves. It was in no such troublous ways that Solomon the all-powerful traversed space and reached the uttermost corners of the earth. Thanks to his great knowledge, he had discovered a means of locomotion compared to which the most magnificent railway coaches and the richest palanquins of Indian princes would seem poor indeed. He had caused his Genii to make a silken carpet of four leagues in extent. In the midst of this carpet was placed a magnificent throne for the royal traveler himself; and around it were seats of gold, of silver, of wood, for the multitude of persons of different rank whom he took with him. There was also no lack of the most gorgeous furniture and the necessary provisions for a king's traveling banquet.

When all was ready Solomon was wont to seat himself upon his throne, and would command the winds to do their duty. Immediately they gently lifted the carpet and bore it rapidly through the air to the appointed spot. During the journey, above the aerial caravan fluttered a cloud of birds, who with their wings formed a splendid canopy to shield their beloved lord from the sun's heat, as the

Hoopoes had first done.

One day, while on such a journey, Solomon was shocked to feel a ray of sunlight piercing through this plumy dais which overhung his head. Shading his eyes, the King glanced up and perceived that there was an opening in the canopy. One bird was missing from its post. In great displeasure Solomon demanded of the Eagle the name of the truant. Anxiously the Eagle called the roll of all the birds in his company; and he was horrified to find that it was Solomon's favorite, the Hoopoe, who was missing. With terror he announced the bird's desertion to the most wise King.

"Soar aloft," commanded Solomon sternly, "and find the Hoopoe that I may punish him. I will pluck off his feathers that he may feel the scorching heat of the sun as his carelessness has caused me to do."

The Eagle soared heavenward, until the earth beneath him looked like a bowl turned upside down. Then he poised on level wings and looked around in every direction to discover the truant. Soon he espied the Hoopoe flying swiftly from the south. The Eagle swooped down and would have seized the culprit roughly in his strong talons, but the Hoopoe begged him for Solomon's sake to be gentle.

"For Solomon's sake!" cried the Eagle. "Do you dare to name the King whom you have injured? He has discovered your absence and in his righteous anger will punish you severely."

"Lead me to him," replied the Hoopoe. "I know that he will forgive me when he hears where I have been and what I have to tell him."

The Eagle led him to the King, who with a wrathful face was sitting on his throne. The Hoopoe trembled and drooped his feathers humbly, but when Solomon would have crushed him in his mighty fist the bird cried,--

"Remember, King, that one day you also must give an account of your sins. Let me not therefore be condemned unheard."

"And if I hear you, what excuse can you have to offer?" answered Solomon, frowning. But this was his favorite bird and he hoped that there might be some reason for sparing him.

"Well," said the Hoopoe, "at Mecca I met a Hoopoe of my acquaintance who told me so wonderful a tale of the marvelous Kingdom of Sheba in Arabia that I could not resist the temptation to visit that country of gold and precious stones. And there, indeed, I saw the most prodigious treasures; but best of all, O King, more glorious than gold, more precious than rare jewels, I saw Queen Balkis, the most beautiful of queens."

"Tell me of this Queen," said Solomon, loosening his rough grasp upon the Hoopoe. So it was, say the Mussulmans, that a bird told Solomon of the great Queen whose journey to Jerusalem is described in the Bible.

The Hoopoe told of her power and glory, her riches, her wisdom, and her beauty, until Solomon sighed a great sigh and said, "It seems too good to be true! But we shall see."

So the King wrote a letter to Balkis, bidding her follow the guidance of fate and come to the court of the wise King. This note he sealed with musk, stamped with his great signet, and gave to the Hoopoe, saying,--

"If now you have spoken truth, take this letter to Queen Balkis; then come away."

The Hoopoe did as he was bid, darting off towards the south like an arrow. And the next day he came to the palace of the Queen of Sheba, where she sat in all her splendor among her counselors. He hopped into the hall and dropped the letter into her lap, then flew away.

Queen Balkis stared and stared at the great King's seal upon the mysterious letter, and when she had read the brief invitation she stared and stared again. But she had heard the fame of Solomon and was eager to ask him some of her clever questions to prove his wisdom. So she decided to accept his invitation and come to Jerusalem.

She came with a great train of attendants, with camels that bore spices and treasures of gold and precious stones, gifts for the most wise King. And she asked him more questions than any woman had ever asked him before, though he knew a great many ladies, and they were all inquisitive.

But Solomon was so wise that he answered all her questions without any trouble.

And she said to him, "It was a true report that I heard of you in my own land, of your wisdom and of your glory. Only that which now I know and see is greater than what I heard. Happy are thy men and happy are thy servants who stand continually before thee and hear thy wisdom."

And she gave the King a hundred and twenty talents of gold, which was a very rich treasure, besides great store of spices, and the most precious gifts; no one had ever seen such gifts as the Queen of Sheba gave to Solomon.

But he in turn was even more generous. For he gave to the fair

Balkis all that she desired and everything she asked, because he admired so much this splendid Queen of whom the Hoopoe had first told him.

And so, the Bible says, the Queen of Sheba turned and went to her own country, she and her servants. But the Mussulmans' tales say that in later days she married Solomon and they lived happily ever after. And it was all the work of that little Hoopoe with a yellow crown, whom after that we may be sure Solomon loved better than ever.

THE PIOUS ROBIN

"Art thou the bird whom man loves best, The pious bird with the scarlet breast, Our little English Robin?" WORDSWORTH.

The English Robin is not precisely like our little American friend whom we call by that name, although, as the lines of poetry quoted above will show, in two ways he is the same as ours: he has a red breast, and he is the bird whom every one loves. Of all the little brothers of the air, in every land and clime, the pretty, jolly, neighborly Robin Redbreast is the favorite.

There are many stories about him: some which tell how he came by his scarlet breast, others which explain why he has always been best beloved of the birds. I have already told how he helped the Wren to bring fire to men. Every one knows how tenderly he covered with leaves the poor Babes in the Wood, when they had been deserted even by their nearest of kin. Some have heard about Saint Kentigern, and how he restored to life the pious Robin of his master Servan,-- the dear little bird who used to sing psalms every morning in the Saint's company. Some also know about the Robin who brought the wheat-ear in his bill to the poor brothers in Brittany who had no grain to plant for their future harvest. All these tales show the

Robin's generous heart, cheerful nature, and pious devotion, which make him beloved by men. But perhaps you do not know why he is called God's own bird.

"The Robin and the Wren Are God's cock and hen,"

sing the little English children, and they think it is very wicked to injure one of the holy birds or make her unhappy by robbing her nest of its pretty eggs.

This is why the Robin is called the good bird, God's bird. The oldest stories say that the little Christ-child used to feed most tenderly the Robins who hopped about the door of His mother's house, for they were dearest of all to His baby heart. Perhaps He thus early learned to love them because His mother had told Him of the service which the dear little birds had once performed for her.

For it is said that once upon a time, when Mary was a little girl, as she was going along the gusty road a bit of straw blew into her eye and pained her terribly. She sat down upon a stone and began to cry. Now a Robin was sitting on a branch close by, singing with all the power of his little throat when the maiden passed, for she was very sweet to see and the Robin loved her looks. But when he saw the blessed Mary begin to cry and rub her eye with her chubby hand, he stopped his gay song and became very sad, wondering what he could do to help her.

What he did was to fly away and tell his friend the Swallow all about it, asking her aid. After that he fluttered to a little fountain which bubbled up close by and brought thence in his bill a drop of water. Then, perching on Mary's forehead, he gently dropped this into the suffering eye. At the same time the Swallow softly brushed her long tail-feathers under the maiden's eyelid, and the hateful straw was wiped away. Thus the little Mary was relieved, and when once more she could look up happily with her pretty eyes she smiled upon the two kind birds and blessed them for their aid.

Of course, if the little Christ heard His mother tell this pretty story He would have been sure to love the Robin, just as she did. And so these little birds became His boyhood friends.

Those were happy times. But in the after years, in the dreadful day when the Saviour was so cruelly done to death by His enemies, the little Robin once more proved his generous and pious heart, so the legends say.

The Saviour hung upon the cross, suffering and sad, while the world was veiled with darkness and all good creatures mourned. Two birds perched upon the cross beside His weary, drooping head. One was the faithful Robin, who was then a plain and dark-colored bird with the scorched feathers of a fire-bringer upon his breast. The other was the Magpie, who at that time was among the most gorgeous and beautiful of all the birds. She had a tuft of bright feathers on her head, and her plumage outshone even that of the Peacock, who has the hundred gleaming eyes of Argus set in his fan-like tail. But the Magpie, in spite of her beauty, was at heart a wicked bird. Think of it! She mocked the dying Saviour in His agony and seemed to rejoice in His suffering!

But the Robin fluttered about the holy figure, timidly uttering chirps of sorrow and longing to help the Master who had fed him tenderly for so many years. With his soft wings he wiped away the tears which flowed from the Lord's eyes, while with his beak he tugged at the cruel thorns which pierced His brow, trying to relieve Him.

Suddenly a drop of blood fell from Christ's forehead upon the Robin's breast and tinged with bright crimson the rusty reddish feathers.

"Blessed be thou," said the Lord, "thou sharer of my suffering. Wherever thou goest happiness and joy shall follow thee. Blue as the heaven shall be thy eggs, and from henceforth thou shalt be the Bird of God, the bearer of good tidings. But thou," He added, addressing the Magpie sorrowfully, "thou art accursed. No longer shall the brilliant tuft and bright feathers of which thou art so proud and so unworthy adorn thee. Thy color shall be the streaked black and white of shadows, thy life a hard one. And thy nest, however well builded, shall be open to the storm."

These were almost the last words which the Saviour spoke. After that, when the Lord was laid in the sepulchre, the faithful Robin still watched beside Him for those three dread days until He rose on Easter morning, when the little bird rejoiced with all nature at the wondrous happening. And again on Ascension Day he paid his last tribute to the risen Master, joining his little song with the chorus of the angels themselves in the gladdest Hosanna which the universe had ever heard.

This explains how the Magpie became a restless, noisy, black-and-white bird as we know her to this day, having lost all her brilliant beauty through the wickedness of her heart. But the pious Robin still wears upon his breast the beautiful feathers stained red with his Master's blood. And all that the Saviour foretold of him has come true. He is the blessed bird whom children everywhere love and of whom they still repeat these old verses:--

"The Robin and the Redbreast, The Robin and the Wren, If ye take out of the nest Ye'll never thrive again. The Robin and the Redbreast, The Martin and the Swallow, If ye touch one of their eggs Bad luck is sure to follow."

THE ROBIN WHO WAS AN INDIAN

The name of Robin makes us think at once of the jolliest and most sociable of all our little brother birds. In every land the name is a favorite, and wherever he goes he brings happiness and kind feeling.

The American Robin is not the same bird as his English cousin, though both have red breasts.

It was in a different manner that our little American friend came to have the ruddy waistcoat which we know so well.

There was a time, so the Indians say, a very early time, long, long before Columbus discovered America,--even before histories began to be written,--when there were no Robins.

In those days in the land of the Ojibways, which is far in the north of the cold country, there lived an old Indian chief who had one son, named Iadilla. Now among the Ojibways, when a boy was almost big enough to become a warrior, before he could go out with the other braves to the hunt or to war, there was a great trial which he must undergo. Other lands and peoples have known similar customs. You remember how, in early Christian times, long, long ago, Galahad and other boys had to fast and watch by their armor during the long night hours before they could become knights, to wear spurs and shield and sword? In just the same way a brown Ojibway lad had to make a long fast in order to win the love of his Guardian Spirit, who would after that watch over him to make him brave and strong. It was a very important event in a boy's life, like graduation from school or college nowadays. For this meant the graduation from boyhood into manhood, the winning of a warrior's diploma.

The father of Iadilla was a brave warrior, a famous chief. But he wished his son to become even better, wiser, greater than he had been. He resolved that the boy should fast longer and harder than ever a lad had fasted before. For he believed that this was the way to make him the noblest of his race. Iadilla was a fine handsome lad, but he was the youngest one who had ever made the trial, and there were many bigger boys than he who were not yet warriors. The other chiefs said that he was not yet old and strong enough.

But Iadilla's father declared that it was time, and bade his son gather courage and pride for the ordeal. "For," he said, "it will be no easy matter, my son, to become the greatest chief of the Ojibways."

"My father," replied Iadilla, humbly, "I will do as you wish. I will do what I can. But my strength is not the strength of the bigger boys; and I think it is yet early to talk of my becoming greatest of the Ojibways. Yet make trial of me, if you wish."

The father of Iadilla had made a little tent of skins where the boy was to live during his fasting time; where he was to lie without food or drink for twelve long days, waiting for a message from the Guardian Spirit whose love was to be the reward of such a trial.

When the time came, the old man led Iadilla to the lodge and bade him lie down on the bed of skins which had been prepared for him. And Iadilla did as he was bid, for he was a brave and obedient lad.

The days crept by, the long, long days of waiting, while Iadilla lay in the lodge bearing hunger and thirst such as no Ojibway lad had ever before known. All day and all night he lay still and spoke never a word. But a dreadful fear was in his heart lest he should not be able to endure the fast for the twelve days which his father had set.

Every morning his father came to the lodge to praise and to encourage him, and to rejoice in one more day checked from the long time of fasting. So eight days passed, and the old man was proud and happy. Already his dear son had done more than any Ojibway lad, and the whole tribe was praising Iadilla, saying what a great chief he would be in the days to come.

But on the ninth morning, when the father peeped into the lodge to see how bravely his son was faring, the boy turned his head toward the door and spoke for the first time in all those long days. He was very thin and pale, and his voice sounded weak.

"My father," he said, "I have slept, and my dreams were sad. I have slept, and my dreams were of failure and weakness. The time does not please my Guardian Spirit. It is not now that I can become a warrior. I am not yet strong and old enough. O my father, I cannot bear the fast longer! I am so hungry, so thirsty, so faint! Let me break my fast, and try again in another year."

But the father sternly refused, for he was ambitious. "Nay, lad," he cried, frowningly. "Would you fail me now? Think of the glory, think of being the greatest of Ojibways. It is but a few short days now. Courage, Iadilla, be a man in strength and patience."

Iadilla said no more. He wrapped himself closer in his blanket and drew his belt tighter about his slender waist, trying to stifle the hunger gnawing there. So he lay silently until the eleventh day. That morning his father came to the lodge, beaming proudly.

"Bravo, my Iadilla!" he cried. "Only one day more, and you will be released from your fast." But Iadilla clasped his hands beseechingly.

"My father," gasped the poor boy. "I cannot bear it another day. I am not fit to be a great chief. I have failed. Give me food, or I die!"

But again the father refused. "It is but a day now," he said, "but a few short hours. Bear a little longer, Iadilla. To-morrow I myself will bring you the finest breakfast that ever a lad ate. Courage, boy, for the few hours that remain."

Iadilla was too weak to answer. He lay motionless, with only a gentle heaving of his breast to show that he still lived. His father left him for the last time, and went to prepare the morrow's goodly breakfast, while the tribe planned a fine festival in honor of the young hero.

Early on the morrow came Iadilla's father to the tent, proudly bearing the breakfast for his brave boy, and smiling to think how gladly he would be received. But he stopped outside the tent door surprised to hear some one talking within. Stooping to a little hole in the skin of the tent he peeped in to find who the speaker might be. Imagine his surprise to find Iadilla standing upright in the middle of the tent painting his breast a brilliant red, as Indians do in war time. And as he daubed on the colors he talked to himself. He spoke softly, yet not with the weak voice of a starving lad; and his face was very beautiful to see, despite its pale thinness.

"My father has ended my Indian life," he said. "My father, too ambitious, has put upon me more than my strength could bear. He would not listen to my prayer of weakness. But I knew, I knew! And my kind Guardian Spirit knew also that it was more than I could bear. He has shown pity, seeing that I was obedient to my father and did my best to please him. Now I am to be no longer an Indian boy. I must take the shape which the Spirit has given me, and go away."

At these strange words the father broke into the tent, exclaiming in terror,--

"My son, my dear son! Do not leave me!"

But, even as he spoke, Iadilla changed into a beautiful Robin

Redbreast with soft feathers and strong, firm wings. And, fluttering up to the ridgepole of the tent, he looked down with pity and tenderness upon the heart-broken chief.

"Do not grieve, father," he sang. "I shall be so much happier as a bird, free from human pain and sorrow. I will cheer you with my merry songs. Oh, I have been hungry; but now I shall get my food so easily, so pleasantly on mountains and in the fields. Oh, once I was thirsty; but now the dew is mine and the little springs. Once I traced my way painfully by forest paths through bog and brake and tangled brier. But now my pathways are in the bright, clear air, where never thorn can tear nor beast can follow. Farewell, dear father! I am so happy!"

He stretched his brown wings as easily as if he had worn them all his life, and, singing a sweet song, fluttered away to the neighboring woods, where he built his nest, and lived happily ever after.

And since that day the glad little Robins have lived as that first one promised, close by the homes of men, and have done all they could to cheer us and make us happy. For they remember how, once upon a time, their ancestor was a human boy.

THE INQUISITIVE WOMAN

There was once a woman who was so very inquisitive that she wished to know everything. She was never happy unless she was poking her nose into some mystery, and the less a matter concerned her the more curious she was about it.

One day the Lord gathered together all the insects in the world, all the beetles, bugs, bees, mosquitoes, ants, locusts, grasshoppers, and other creatures who fly or hop or crawl, and shut them up in a huge sack well tied at the end. What a queer, squirming, muffled-buzzing bundle it made, to be sure!

Then the Lord called the woman to him and said, "Woman, I would have you take this sack and throw it into the sea. But be sure and do not untie the end of it to look inside; for the sack must on no account be opened, even for a single minute."

The woman took the sack, wondering very much at the queer size and shape and feeling of it, and especially at the strange noises which came from the inside.

"What can be in the sack?" she said to herself. "Oh, I wish I knew! Oh, how I wish I knew! Oh, how very, very much I wish I knew!" Her curiosity increased every minute as she went step by step towards the sea, until when she had gone scarcely a hundred paces she stopped short and said, "I must know what is inside this sack before I go any farther. I will take just one tiny little peep, and He will never know it."

Very carefully she untied the neck of the sack. Buzz! Whirr! Hum! Zim! She had opened it but a tiny little crack when out crawled and hopped and flew the millions and swarms and colonies of all kinds of insects, and away they scattered in every direction. Such a noise as filled the air about the astonished woman's head! Such a wriggling and squirming and hopping in the grass about her feet!

"Oh, now I know what was in the sack!" she cried. "But I wish I had not looked. Oh, whatever shall I do? He told me to throw the bag into the ocean without looking in. But now the horrid creatures have escaped everywhere and He will know what I have done. Oh, what will He do to punish me?"

She began to run hither and yon like a crazy woman, picking up the bugs and jumping for the fluttering insects, trying to put them back into the bag. They stung her and bit her and got into her eyes until she screamed with pain. As fast as she caught one another escaped, and she soon saw that it was a hopeless task. She could never catch the millions of creatures who had scattered away to their homes in every corner of the world.

Then the Lord came to her and said very sternly, "O Woman, you have disobeyed me, just as did the very first woman of all. And you must be punished both for your disobedience and for your inquisitiveness which has led you into the worse sin. Not until you have gathered up every one of these insects which you have permitted to escape back into the world shall you be happy. But I will give you wings to help you in the task. You shall become a Woodpecker, and it shall be your task to hunt, hunt for the insects which hide away so slyly at your approach. Not till the last one of these is gobbled up from the earth shall you return to your own shape and be a woman once more."

Then the Lord changed the inquisitive woman into a restless Woodpecker, and with a "tut-tut!" she darted away in pursuit of the insects which had brought her into such trouble.

And that is why to this day one sees the Woodpecker pecking so frantically on the tree trunks, anxious lest a single insect should escape. For she is very tired of being a bird, and is longing to become a woman once more. But it will be a very long time, I fear, before she gathers up all the wriggling, squirming, hopping, buzzing, stinging, biting things that make life in the country so varied, exciting, and musical.

WHY THE NIGHTINGALE WAKES

When the other birds are sound asleep in their nests, with their little heads tucked comfortably under their feathers, Sister Nightingale, they say, may not rest, but still sounds the notes of her beautiful song in grove and thicket.

Why does she sing thus, all night long as well as through the day? It is because she dares not go to sleep on account of the Blindworm, who is waiting to catch her with her eyes closed.

Once upon a time, when the world was very new, the Blindworm was not quite blind, but had one good eye. Moreover, in those days the Nightingale also had but one eye. As for the Blindworm, it mattered very little; for he was a homely creature, content to crawl about in the dark underground, or under wood and leaves, where nobody saw him and nobody cared. But the Nightingale's case was really quite too pitiful! Fancy the sweetest singer among all the birds, the favorite chorister, going about with but one eye, while every one else, even the tiniest little Humming Bird of all, had two.

The Nightingale felt very sore about this matter, and tried to conceal her misfortune from the other birds. She managed to cock her head the other way whenever she met a friend, and she always flew past any stranger so fast that he never saw the empty socket where her other pretty eye should be.

But one day there was great excitement among the birds. Miss Jenny Wren was going to be married to young Cock Robin. There was to be a grand wedding; every one was invited, and of course the Nightingale was needed to lead the bridal chorus of feathered songsters. But the poor Nightingale was set in a flutter of anxiety by the news.

"Oh, dear me!" she said, "I do want to go to Jenny's wedding, oh, of course I do! But how can I go? If I do, the other birds will discover that I have but one eye, and then how the disagreeable creatures will laugh at me. Oh dear, oh dear! What shall I do? I cannot go, no, I really cannot. But what excuse can I give? Oh, it is not right that the sweetest singer in all Birdland should be laughed at, merely because she has the misfortune to lack one poor little eye!"

The Nightingale sat on the branch, singing so mournfully that all the creatures on the ground below went sorrowfully about their daily business. Just then the Nightingale spied a silvery gleam among the dead leaves. It was the Blindworm, a spotted gray streak, writhing noiselessly along towards the decayed wood of a fallen tree, in which he loved to burrow. And the Blindworm was not sad like the others, neither seemed he to care in the least about the Nightingale's music. Worms think little of sweet sounds. He cocked his one eye up towards the Nightingale and winked maliciously. He alone of all creatures knew the Nightingale's secret.

"Good-day, Sister Nightingale," he said. "How is your eye this morning? We have a goodly pair between us; though I think that mine is rather the better of the two."

Then he disappeared into a tiny opening. For though the Blindworm is nearly a foot long he is so smooth and slippery that he can enter a hole which is almost smaller than himself.

The Nightingale was very indignant at being addressed in this familiar way by a miserable, crawling creature who not only could not fly, but who could not sing a note, and did not know do from fa. Besides, it made her angry to think that he knew her secret and talked aloud about it so that any one might hear.

"The idea!" she cried. "It is bad enough that I cannot go to the wedding of my dear friend Jenny. But to be jeered at by this creature, it is more than I can bear. Ha! I have an idea. I will punish him and help myself at the same time. I will steal his one eye and wear it to Jenny Wren's wedding; then no one will ever discover my misfortune."

Now this was an excellent scheme, but it was not so easy to carry it out as the Nightingale had thought. For the Blindworm was very timid and kept himself carefully hidden in his burrow of soft soil, as if he half suspected the Nightingale's plans. Day after day the Nightingale kept eager watch upon his movements, and at last, on the very eve of the wedding, when she had almost given up hope, she spied the Blindworm sound asleep on the moss under a tall tree.

"Ha!" said the Nightingale to herself very softly. "Now is my chance!" She fluttered into the top of the oak tree, and from there hopped down from branch to branch, from twig to twig, until she was directly over the sleeper's ugly head, over the one closed eye. Then whirr! Down she pounced upon the Blindworm. And before the creature had a chance to know what was happening, the Nightingale had stolen his eye, and had popped it into place in the empty socket on the other side of her beak.

"Ha, ha!" she sang merrily. "Now I have two bright eyes, as good as any one's. Now I can go to Jenny Wren's wedding as gayly as I please, and no one shall see more of the ceremony than I. I shall be able to tell just exactly how the bride is dressed, how every little feather is arranged, and how she looks after Parson Crow has pronounced the blessing. Oh, how happy I am!"

But the poor Blindworm, blind indeed from that day forth, began to cry and lament, begging the Nightingale to give him back his eye.

"Nay," said the Nightingale, "did you not laugh at me when you saw me sadly sitting on the tree, mourning because I could not go to the wedding? Now I have stolen your eye, and I can see famously. But you will never again see me sitting sadly on the tree."

Then the Blindworm grew very angry. "I will get the eye back!" he cried. "I will steal it from you, as you stole it from me, some time when you are asleep. I will climb up into your nest some night, and I will take both your eyes of which you are so proud. Then you will be blind, wholly blind as I am now."

At these threatening words the Nightingale ceased to sing and became silent with fear. For she knew that the Blindworm would do as he said. But again a brilliant thought came to her.

"Nay!" she trilled gladly. "That you shall never do. I will never sleep again. I will keep awake always, night and day, with my two bright eyes ever looking out for danger. Yes, yes, yes! No one shall ever catch me napping."

"You cannot help yourself," said the Blindworm. "You cannot keep awake. You will drowse in spite of everything. I shall yet find you asleep some night, and then beware!"

"Nay, nay!" warbled the Nightingale, as she flew away to make herself fine for the wedding. "I shall sing, sing, sing night and day henceforth to keep myself awake. And thus I need not fear. Farewell-well-well!"

And so the Nightingale went to the wedding and sang more sweetly in the bridal chorus than she had ever sung before. And after that, although she was weary, oh, so weary! she sang all night long, and all the next night and the next. And so she has continued to sing ever since in the lands which are blessed by her presence. For she dares not go to sleep even for a single moment, knowing that the Blindworm is ever ready to pounce upon her and take away the eyes which she is now enjoying.

MRS. PARTRIDGE'S BABIES

Long, long ago, when the world was very young indeed, the Birds and Animals used to send their children to school, to Mother Magpie's kindergarten. All the morning long the babies learned their lessons which it was needful for them to know. And when the noon hour came their various mammas came to the school bringing lunches for the children. You can imagine how gladly they were received by the hungry little scholars.

One day Mrs. Partridge was very busy with her house-cleaning, and when the noontime came she could not leave her work to go to the school with her babies' lunch.

"Dear me," she said, looking out of the nest, "here it is noon and the little Partridges will be so very hungry. But I really cannot leave home now. What shall I do? If only some other mamma were going that way."

She craned her neck and looked eagerly in every direction. And finally she spied Madame Tortoise plodding along towards the school, with the lunch for her little Turtlets.

"Oho, neighbor, oho! Stop a minute!" cried Mrs. Partridge, waving a wing at Tortoise. "Are you going schoolward, as I think? Oh, dear Madame Tortoise, if you knew how busy I am to-day. I don't think any one was ever so busy as I am with my house-cleaning. Will you do me a favor, please?"

The Tortoise sniffed. "Well, I am a busy woman myself," she said, "but I am willing to oblige a neighbor. What is it you wish, ma'am?"

"Oh, thank you so much!" cried the Partridge. "Dear Madame Tortoise, I shall never forget your kindness. Now, will you take this bunch of nice wiggly worms to my little ones for their lunch? I shall be so very grateful."

"Don't mention it," snapped the Tortoise, who was rather tired of hearing Mrs. Partridge's shrill thanks. "I'm perfectly willing to take the lunch, since I am going to the same place. But I don't know your babies. What do they look like, ma'am?"

"Oh, that is easily told," cried Mrs. Partridge. "They are the most beautiful little creatures in the school. They are said greatly to resemble me. You will have no trouble in recognizing them. When you come to the school just look around at all the children, and pick out the three most beautiful of all. Those are certain to be mine. Give them the wiggly worms, please, with my love. And oh, thank you, Madame Tortoise, so very much! Some time I will do as much for you. So neighborly! Thank you!"

"Don't mention it!" snapped the Tortoise again, very much bored by all this chatter. She sniffed as she moved slowly along towards the school, with the second lunch carried carefully on her broad shell-back. "They are nice fat worms," she said.

Now when the Tortoise came to the school it was high noon, and all the children were waiting open-mouthed for their mammas and the lunches which they expected. Such rows and rows of wide hungry mouths! Madame Tortoise moved slowly up and down and round and round, eyeing the various children who begged for the nice wiggly worms. "H'm!" she said to herself, "hungry children seem to look considerably alike, and none of them are so wondrously beautiful when their mouths are wide open greedily. I wonder which are Mrs. Partridge's children. She told me to give this lunch to the handsomest babies here. Well, I will, and if I make a mistake it will not be my fault. Hello! Here are my dear little Turtlets! Bless the babies, how pretty they are! Why, I declare, I never realized that they were so handsome. Certainly, they are the best-looking children in the school. Then I must give them Mrs. Partridge's luncheon, for so I promised. Yes, my little ones, here is your lunch which I brought for you. And when you have finished that, here is another, some nice, fat, wiggly worms which mother collected on the way,--a prize for the handsomest children in the school."

So the little Turtlets fared wonderfully well that day; but the poor little Partridges went hungry, and had dreadful headaches, and went home peeping sadly to their silly mother. And Mrs. Partridge had no more sense than to be angry with Madame Tortoise, which I think was very unfair, don't you? For the latter had only done as she was bidden by her silly and conceited neighbor.

But after that the Tortoise and the Partridge never spoke to each other, and their children would not play together at school.

THE EARLY GIRL

There were once two girls who were very dear friends, Zada and Tourtourelle. One morning Zada woke up and said, "O Tourtourelle! Last night I had such a strange dream!"

"And so did I!" cried Tourtourelle. "Let us tell each other the dreams. But you first, Zada."

Zada began to laugh. "I dreamed I was a pretty bird with a tuft of feathers on my head. I could fly, and, O Tourtourelle! it was great fun! But the most amusing thing of all was that I could sing so finely, and mock all the birds of the forest. Nay, I could even imitate the sounds of animals. I cannot help laughing when I think what a jolly time I had."

"Why, Zada!" cried Tourtourelle, wondering, "I dreamed the very same thing. I too was a pretty little bird, and I too could imitate all kinds of sounds as I fluttered in the tree-tops. Surely, the dream will come true for one of us. How fine that would be!"

"Yes, let it be for the one of us who first rises to-morrow morning," said Zada. And so the two friends agreed.

Now when it came night-time Zada went to bed very early, like a wise little girl who wants to rise with the sun. But Tourtourelle said to herself, "I know what I will do, I will not go to sleep. I will sit up all night, and then I am sure to be the first to rise."

So Tourtourelle perched herself on a high-backed chair and stretched her eyes wide open. For hours and hours she sat there, growing more sleepy every minute. Towards morning she began to nod; she could hardly keep her eyes open, though she tried to prop the lids with her finger tips. Finally, whether she would or no, she fell fast asleep, poor little Tourtourelle, worn out with her long vigil.

When the first morning sunbeam peeped into the chamber Zada opened her eyes, refreshed and smiling. She sat up in bed remembering the dream, and then jumped lightly to the floor. As she did so she glanced at her feet, which felt queer. Wonderful! They were little bird claws! She looked down at herself. She was covered with soft feathers. She tried to move her arms, and when she did so she rose lightly from the floor and skimmed out of the window into the garden. Zada had become a pretty little bird, just as she had dreamed. Oh, how happy she was! She heard a Lark singing far up in the sky. Opening her mouth, she warbled and trilled as well as he, until he dropped down quickly to the earth, thinking it must be his mate who sang so sweetly. She spied a Chicken strayed too far from the mother Hen; and chuckling to herself mischievously she imitated the warning cry of a Hawk, till the Chick ran squawking back to the shelter of his mother's wing. She heard a hound baying afar off, and with little trouble echoed the sound so perfectly that a groom came running out of the stable, whistling for the dog which he feared was straying from the kennel. Zada found that as in her dream she could imitate all the sounds which she heard; and she was so pleased that she sang and sang and sang, hopping from tree to tree, teasing the other birds with her mockery, and puzzling them, too.

As for poor Tourtourelle, when she waked it was very late. She yawned and rubbed her eyes languidly, for she was still sleepy. Then looking across to Zada's bed she saw that it was empty. Her heart gave a great thump, for she longed and longed to be a bird, but now she feared that she was too late. In her white gown she ran out into the garden looking for Zada. But first she saw an old man leading his cow to the pasture. And to the cow he said, "Coo-roo, coo-roo!" coaxing her to hasten.

"Coo-roo, coo-roo!" cried Tourtourelle, imitating him, she knew not why. And as she said it she wondered at the strange feeling which came over her. For her body felt very light and it seemed as if she could fly. She looked down and saw that she was no longer covered with a little white gown but with soft feathers of ashy gray, while wings sprouted from her shoulders.

"Oh, I have become a bird!" she tried to say, but all she uttered was--"Coo-roo, coo-roo!" For Tourtourelle was become a beautiful Turtle-Dove, and that is all a Turtle-Dove can say.

"Coo-roo, coo-roo!" mocked a voice from the tree. And cocking her little reddish eye Tourtourelle saw a brilliant Jay hopping in the branches, imitating a Dove. Then it was the song of a Wren that she heard, then a Lark, then a Thrush, then a Sparrow-Hawk,--all these sounds coming from the one little throat of the happy bird on that bough. Tourtourelle tried to do likewise, but all she could sing was "Coo-roo! coo-roo!" And she said mournfully to herself:--

"It is Zada. She was wiser than I, and earlier, and the dream came true for her. Oh dear! Oh dear!" And to this day Turtle-Dove flies about sadly uttering her monotonous cry, and listening with a longing that would be envy, were she not so good a little bird, to the chatter of her friend the Jay.

For Zada the Jay is always merry, hopping from tree to tree, playing her jokes upon the other birds whom she deceives with her wonderful voice. And she leads a life so gay and exciting that she never finds time to be sad, even over the disappointment of her dear friend, poor little Tourtourelle.

HOW THE BLACKBIRD SPOILED HIS COAT

Once upon a time, our friend Blackbird, who comes first of the feathered brothers in the spring, was not black at all. No, indeed; he was white--white as feather-snow new fallen in the meadow. There are very few birds who have been thought worthy to dress all in beautiful white, for that is the greatest honor which a bird can have. So, like the Swan and the Dove, Master Whitebird--for that is what they called him then--was very proud of his spotless coat.

He was very proud and happy, and he sang all day long, the jolliest songs. But you see he did not really deserve this honor, because he was at heart a greedy bird; and therefore a great shame came upon him, and after that he was never proud nor happy any more. I shall tell you the story of how the Whitebird grew grimy and gloomy as we know him, almost as black and solemn as old Daddy Crow.

Once upon a time, then, Master Whitebird was teetering on a rose-bush, ruffling his beautiful white feathers and singing little bits of poetry about himself to any one who would listen.

"Ho-ho, ho-hee, Just look at me!"

he piped, and cocked his little eyes about in every direction, to see who might be admiring his wondrous whiteness.

But all on a sudden his song gurgled down into his throat and choked itself still, and his eyes fixed themselves upon a tree close by. It was a dead old tree, and there was a hole in the trunk halfway up to the lowest limb, a round little hole about as big as your two fists.

Whitebird had seen something black pop into that hole in a sly and secret way, and he began to wonder; for he was inquisitive, as most birds are. He sat quite still on his rose-bush and watched and watched. Presently out of the hole popped a black head, bigger than Whitebird's, with two wise little twinkling eyes.

"Oho!" said Whitebird to himself, "it is Mother Magpie up to her old tricks, hiding, hiding. Maybe she has a treasure hidden there. I will watch, and perhaps I shall find out something worth knowing."

Mother Magpie was the wisest and the slyest of all the birds, and it was always worth while, as Whitebird knew, to take lessons of her. So he sat perfectly still until she came cautiously back carrying something in her beak. It was round and white and glinted like moonlight. Whitebird's eyes stuck out greedily.

"It is a piece of silver!" he thought, but he sat perfectly still until the Magpie had stowed the coin safely in the hollow tree and had hopped away as if upon an unfinished errand. "Aha! there is more then. I will watch to see what comes next," said Whitebird. And he waited.

Sure enough. In a little while the Magpie returned, this time bringing something which glowed yellow like sunlight.

"It is a piece of gold!" gasped Whitebird, and his eyes bulged out like those of lobsters, he was so jealous of her luck. But he silently watched her disappear into her tree-cupboard and then hastily depart as before toward the mountain. "What comes next?" muttered Whitebird to himself. "I am dying to peep into that hole. I cannot wait much longer."

Then, after a while, a third time came back the Magpie to the dead tree. And lo, what she carried in her beak twinkled and trembled and shone in many colors, like a drop of dew on a velvet flower-cheek. When Whitebird saw this sight, he nearly tumbled off his perch with excitement.

"It is a diamond!" he cried aloud; "oh, it is a real diamond!"

At this sudden noise from the rose-bush Mother Magpie's nerves were so shocked that she dropped the diamond helter-skelter into the hole. And in a moment she fell in after it, out of sight. She hoped that no one had seen her, but little Whitebird knew the place. He hopped after her and, perching on the edge of the hole, peered down into the hollow tree. And there he saw a great heap of silver and gold and precious stones, which Mother Magpie was trying to cover with her wings.

"Oh, what a treasure! What a treasure!" he piped greedily. "Mother Magpie, you must tell me where you found it, that I may go and get some for myself."

But Mother Magpie refused to tell.

"Oho!" chirped Whitebird, angrily; "we shall see about that! Then I will call in the fierce birds, Robber Hawk and Fighting Falcon and the bloody Butcher Bird, and they will take your treasure from you, and kill you, too, into the bargain. What do you think of that, Mother

Magpie?"

Then she was afraid, for she knew those bad birds; and she saw that she must trust her secret with Whitebird, since he had already discovered half the truth.

"Well, if you will promise me not to let any one else know, not even King Eagle, I will tell you," she said. So Whitebird promised.

"Listen," said the Magpie. "You must find the cave which is near the tallest oak on the mountain, under the flat stone. In a corner there is a tiny hole, just big enough for you or me to pass. And this is the entrance to a passage which leads down into the cellars of the earth. And when you have gone down and down, farther than any one except myself ever went before, you will come to the palace of the King of Riches. It is full of gold and silver and precious stones like these you see here. Each chamber is more beautiful and more tempting than the last. But you must not touch a stone or a single coin, or even a little bit of gold-dust, until you have seen the King. For first you must offer yourself to be his servant, and then he will be generous; then he will let you carry away as much treasure as your beak will hold. That is all there is to it. But beware, greedy Whitebird! Take my advice, and do not touch a grain of treasure before you see the King, or great evil will befall you."

Whitebird promised to do as she said. And then away he flew to the blue mountain and its tallest oak. Close by the great oak, in a lonely spot, he found the flat rock, and under it was the cave where once a bear had lived. Whitebird hopped in eagerly, and away back in one corner of the cave he found a little round hole, as the Magpie had said; a hole not much bigger than an apple. It must have been a tight squeeze for fat Mother Magpie!

Whitebird hopped through the hole and found himself in a long, narrow passage which led down, down, down into places where his eyes were of no use at all. For he was not like Master Owl, who can see better in the dark than anywhere else. Blindly he hopped on and on, till he came into a great cavern, bright with a white radiance, as if the moonlight filtered in from somewhere. It was the first room of the King's palace of treasure; and it was all of silver, paved with silver, heaped with silver, shining with silver. Whitebird's eyes glittered and he wanted to stop and take some for himself. But just in time he remembered the wise warning of Mother Magpie; and so he hopped on over the silver pebbles through a silver door into a second room. And this was flooded with yellow light as of sunshine, so dazzling that for a moment Whitebird's yellow eyes could see nothing at all. When he could see, the place seemed full of yellow eyes like his own, great yellow eyes heaped up from floor to ceiling. And when he became used to this he looked again and saw that these were golden coins, and that this was a cavern all of gold.

Oh, such a wonderful sight! Oh, such a golden dream! The floor on which he stood was deep with gold dust, which squished between his toes like yellow sand on a sea beach. And then Whitebird lost his head and went quite mad, forgetting the words of wise Mother Magpie.

"Gold dust, gold dust, a treasure for me!" he sang, hopping up and down on one leg. "I can carry away a great beakful of the yellow seeds, and each one will blossom into a golden flower for me--for me--for me!" He was wholly crazy, as you see.

He thrust his bill deep into the gold dust of the floor, and greedily filled it more than full, till it dropped over his white, white feathers and splashed his coat so that he was no longer a white bird but a yellow bird. Oh, the silly, greedy thing! But there are worse fates than being a yellow bird.

Just at this moment a dreadful roar echoed through the caverns till they rumbled like an earthquake, and into the golden chamber crashed a horrible dragon-creature, the guardian of the King's treasure. His eyes blazed red like coals, and from his mouth came smoke and flame so that the gold melted before his breath. He rushed straight upon poor little Whitebird to gobble him up, and as he came he roared: "Thief, thief! who steals my master's treasure? I scorch you with my eye! I burn you with my breath! I swallow you into the furnace of my throat. Gr-r-r-r!"

There seemed no chance for Whitebird to escape, the creature was so near. But with a cry of terror he fluttered and hopped away as fast as he could toward the narrow passage, through the gold chamber and the silver chamber, leaving all the treasure behind. (Oh, don't you wish we could have known how the diamond chamber looked, with its rainbow light?)

Whitebird hopped and fluttered, fluttered and hopped, feeling the dragon's hot breath close behind frizzling his feathers and blinding his eyes with smoke. He seemed like to be roasted alive in this horrible underground oven. But oh, there was the hole close before him! Pouf! With a terrible roar the dragon snapped at him as Whitebird popped through the hole; but he got only a mouthful of burnt tail-feathers. Whitebird was safe, safe in the narrow passage where the dragon could not follow. Up and up and up and up he feebly fluttered into the light of the dear outside world, and then he gave a chirp of joy to find that he really had escaped. But oh, how tired and frightened he was!

Mother Magpie was sitting on a bush waiting for him, for she had guessed what would happen to the greedy bird. And when she saw him she gave a squawk of laughter.

"O Whitebird," she chuckled, "what a sight! what a sight! Your lovely coat, your spotless feathers! Oh, you greedy, greedy Blackbird!"

Then he who had been Whitebird looked down at himself and saw what a dreadful thing had happened. And he closed his eyes and gave a hoarse, sad croak. For the smoke and flame of the dragon's breath had smirched and scorched him from top to toe, so that he was no longer white, but thenceforth and forever Blackbird.

I think Mother Magpie must have told the story to her children, chuckling over the greedy fellow's failure. And they told it to the children of sunny France, from whom I got the tale for you. So now you know why the Blackbird looks so solemn and so sulky in his suit of rusty black; and why his nerves are so weak that if one suddenly surprises him, picking up seeds in the field, he gives a terrible scream of fright. For he thinks one is that dreadful dragon-creature who chased him and so nearly gobbled him on that unlucky day, long ago.

Poor Brother Blackbird! Don't let him know I told you all this; it would make him so very much ashamed.

THE BLACKBIRD AND THE FOX

One day Madame Fox, who was strolling along under the hedge, heard a Blackbird trilling on a branch. Quick as thought she jumped and seized the little fellow, and was about to gobble him down then and there. But the Blackbird began to chirp piteously:--

"Oh, oh, Madame Fox! What are you thinking of? Just see, I am such a tiny mouthful! And when I am gone--I am gone. Only let me free and I will tell you something. Look! Here come some peasant women with eggs and cheese which they are carrying to the market at Verrilles. That would be a meal worth having! Only let me go, and

I will help you, Master Fox."

The Fox saw that this might be a good plan which the bird proposed, so she let him go.

And what do you think the Blackbird did? He began to hop, hop, hop toward the women, dragging his wing behind him as if it were broken, which is a trick some birds know very well.

"Look!" cried one of the women, when she caught sight of him. "Oh, look at the little Blackbird there! His wing is broken and he cannot fly. I shall try to catch him." And she ran as fast as she could, making her hands into a little cage to put over him. The other women, too, set down their baskets, for convenience--set them down right in the middle of the road--and joined the chase after the poor little Blackbird, so lame, so lame! But always, as they came close to him, he managed to flutter out of reach.

Meanwhile, Madame Fox went round about by the hedge and came all quietly and unseen to the place where the baskets waited in the road. And oh! what a good dinner she found there; chickens and eggs and fresh cheese nicely done up for the market. And the greedy old lady ate them all--all the chickens and the eggs and the cheeses. My! How fat she was when all was done.

Now the Blackbird hopped on and on for a long, long way, until, by cocking his eye, he saw that Madame Fox had finished her dinner. And then, houff! Up he flew, with a jolly chirp of laughter, right over the heads of the astonished women. What of his broken wing now? He began to whistle, to sing, to chirrup like a crazy bird up there in the air. The women looked at one another sheepishly.

"Ah, the wicked Blackbird!" they said. "One would have thought that he could not fly at all. But look at him, the sly creature! Oho, it is a pretty trick he has played us!"

They turned back to where they had left their baskets, intending to start on for the market. But when they came there--well, well! What a shame!--they found the eggs, the chickens, the cheeses all gone-- eaten up by the greedy Fox. And then they began to scold and cry.

"Oh, what misfortune!" they wailed. "We have lost our eggs, our chickens, and our cheeses, and there is nothing left to carry to market. We have not even a Blackbird to show for our morning's work. Oh dear! oh dear! It is all the fault of that wicked, deceitful little bird."

And, instead of going on to Verrilles, they turned about with their empty baskets and went back home, a sorry party, scolding and crying all the way. But long before they reached their homes and their angry husbands Madame Fox was comfortably snoozing her after-dinner nap under the hedge; while the happy Blackbird picked up juicy bugs in the neighboring meadow, with one eye cocked to guard against being surprised a second time by any bushy-tailed rogue.

THE DOVE WHO SPOKE TRUTH

The Dove and the wrinkled little Bat once went on a journey together. When it came towards night a storm arose, and the two companions sought everywhere for a shelter. But all the birds were sound asleep in their nests and the animals in their holes and dens. They could find no welcome anywhere until they came to the hollow tree where old Master Owl lived, wide awake in the dark.

"Let us knock here," said the shrewd Bat, "I know the old fellow is not asleep. This is his prowling hour, and but that it is a stormy night he would be abroad hunting.--What ho, Master Owl!" he squeaked, "will you let in two storm-tossed travelers for a night's lodging?"

Gruffly the selfish old Owl bade them enter, and grudgingly invited them to share his supper. The poor Dove was so tired that she could scarcely eat, but the greedy Bat's spirits rose as soon as he saw the viands spread before him. He was a sly fellow, and immediately began to flatter his host into good humor. He praised the Owl's wisdom and his courage, his gallantry and his generosity; though every one knew that however wise old Master Owl might be, he was neither brave nor gallant. As for his generosity,--both the Dove and the Bat well remembered his selfishness towards the poor Wren, when the Owl alone of all the birds refused to give the little fire-bringer a feather to help cover his scorched and shivering body.

All this flattery pleased the Owl. He puffed and ruffled himself, trying to look as wise, gallant, and brave as possible. He pressed the Bat to help himself more generously to the viands, which invitation the sly fellow was not slow to accept.

During this time the Dove had not uttered a word. She sat quite still staring at the Bat and wondering to hear such insincere speeches of flattery. Suddenly the Owl turned to her.

"As for you, Miss Pink-eyes," he said gruffly, "you keep careful silence. You are a dull table-companion. Pray, have you nothing to say for yourself?"

"Yes," exclaimed the mischievous Bat, "have you no words of praise for our kind host? Methinks he deserves some return for this wonderfully generous, agreeable, tasteful, well-appointed, luxurious, elegant, and altogether acceptable banquet. What have you to say, O little Dove?"

But the Dove hung her head, ashamed of her companion, and said very simply:--

"O Master Owl, I can only thank you with all my heart for the hospitality and shelter which you have given me this night. I was beaten by the storm, and you took me in. I was hungry, and you gave me your best to eat. I cannot flatter nor make pretty speeches like the Bat. I never learned such manners. But I thank you."

"What!" cried the Bat, pretending to be shocked. "Is that all you have to say to our obliging host? Is he not the wisest, bravest, most gallant and generous of gentlemen? Have you no praise for his noble character as well as for his goodness to us? I am ashamed of you! You do not deserve such hospitality. You do not deserve this shelter."

The Dove remained silent. Like Cordelia in the play, she could not speak untruths even for her own happiness.

"Truly, you are an unamiable guest," snarled the Owl, his yellow eyes growing keen and fierce with anger and mortified pride. "You are an ungrateful bird, Miss, and the Bat is right. You do not deserve this generous hospitality which I have offered, this goodly shelter which you asked. Away with you! Leave my dwelling! Pack off into the storm and see whether or not your silence will soothe the rain and the wind. Be off, I say!"

"Yes, away with her!" echoed the Bat, flapping his leathery wings. And the two heartless creatures fell upon the poor little Dove and drove her out into the dark and stormy night.

Poor little Dove! All night she was tossed and beaten about shelterless in the storm, because she had been too truthful to flatter the vain old Owl. But when the bright morning dawned, draggled and weary as she was, she flew to the court of King Eagle and told him all her trouble. Great was the indignation of that noble bird.

"For his flattery and his cruelty let the Bat never presume to fly abroad until the sun goes down," he cried. "As for the Owl, I have already doomed him to this punishment for his treatment of the Wren. But henceforth let no bird have anything to do with either of them, the Bat or the Owl. Let them be outcasts and night-prowlers, enemies to be attacked and punished if they appear among us, to be avoided by all in their loneliness. Flattery and inhospitality, deceit and cruelty,--what are more hideous than these? Let them cover themselves in darkness and shun the happy light of day. As for you, little Dove, let this be a lesson to you to shun the company of flatterers, who are sure to get you into trouble. But you shall always be loved for your simplicity and truth. And as a token of our affection your name shall be used by poets as long as the world shall last to rhyme with love."

The words of the wise King Eagle are true to this day. So now you know why a great many poems came to be written in which the rhymes dove and love have not seemed to make any particular sense.

THE FOWLS ON PILGRIMAGE

Once upon a time old Lady Fox was very hungry, but she had nothing to eat, and there was no sign of a dinner to be had anywhere.

"What shall I do, what shall I do?" whined the Fox. "I am so faint and hungry, but all the birds and all the fowls are afraid of me and will not venture near enough for me to consult them about a dinner. I have so bad a name that no one will trust me. What can I do to win back the respect of the community and earn a square meal? Ah, I have it! I will turn pious and go upon a pilgrimage. That ought to make me popular once more."

So the Fox started upon the pilgrimage. She had not gone very far when she met a Cock, but he knew the character of Madame Fox too well to trust himself near. He flew up into a tree, and from that safe perch crowed jauntily, "Good morning, Madame Fox. Whither away so fast?"

The Fox drew down the corners of her mouth, trying to look pious, and rolled up her eyes as she answered in a hollow voice, "Oh, Master Cock, I am going on a pious pilgrimage. I am sorry for my wicked life, and now I am going to be good."

"Ah," said the Cock, "I am indeed glad to hear that! Going on a pilgrimage, are you? Well, in that case I will go with you."

"Do, Master Cock, do," answered the Fox fervently. "It will do you good. Come sit upon my broad back and I will carry you."

The Cock thanked her and climbed upon her back, and so they proceeded on their pilgrimage together. After a while they came upon a Dove, which fluttered away hastily when she saw old Lady Fox, knowing too well her wicked tricks. But the Fox called to her in a gentle voice:--

"Do not be afraid, O Dove. I know why you start at my approach. But I have repented of my former sins and have turned pilgrim. My friend, the Cock, and I have just started upon our pious journey. Will you join us?"

When the innocent Dove saw the Cock upon the Fox's back she thought that certainly everything must be safe, so she answered:--

"Yes, Madame Fox, I will go with you."

"Jump right up on my back; there is plenty of room beside the Cock," said the Fox cordially.

A little further on they met a wild Duck, who waddled away quacking wildly when he saw the Fox trotting towards him. But the sly old lady called out to him, smiling:--

"Be calm, little brother. I have given up my former unkind tricks, for which I sadly repent, and now I am going on a pious pilgrimage. See, your friends the Cock and the Dove are my companions."

"In that case I will go along, too," said the Duck, "for you have a goodly party."

"That is right," replied the Fox approvingly. "I thought you would go. Kindly take a back seat with the others."

Now when these queer pilgrims had traveled for some time they came to a cave in the rocks, a deep dark cave which looked like a den. And here the Fox stopped, saying:--

"Dear brothers, it is time that we paused and thought more carefully about our sins. We must cross seas and rivers, and Heaven knows when we shall reach the end of our journey. Let us listen to one another's confessions, for I am sure we have all been miserable sinners. Come, Mr. Cock, come into the cave with me and I will hear you first."

The Cock followed her into the cave, saying with some surprise, "Why, Madame Fox, what have I done that is wicked?"

"Do you not know?" answered the Fox sternly. "Why, do you not begin to crow at midnight and wake poor tired people out of their first sleep? Go to! You ought to be ashamed! Then again you crow at the most inconveniently early hour in the morning and make the caravans mistake the true time, so that they start upon their journeys long before the proper hour and fall into the hands of robbers who prowl about before light. These are dreadful sins, Mr. Cock, and you deserve to be punished." So the wicked old Fox seized the Cock and ate him all up.

After the Fox had finished him she came to the entrance of the cave and called, "Now you come, little Dove, and tell me what you have done that is naughty."

"But I have done nothing," said the innocent Dove, wondering very much; "of what evil do you accuse me, Madame Fox?"

"When the farmers sow their grain you dig up the yellow kernels and eat them for your dinner. That is stealing, which is a wicked, wicked sin, and must be severely punished," cried the hungry Fox. And thereupon she seized the poor little Dove and ate her up.

Once more the Fox stood at the door of the cave, stealthily licking her chops, and she called out to the Duck, "Come in, Mr. Duck, and I will hear what you have to say."

"Well, I have not done anything wrong," said the Duck positively, "and you cannot say that I have; can you now, Madame Fox?"

"Oh, indeed and indeed!" exclaimed the Fox. "Have you not stolen the king's gold crown, and do you not wear it on your head, you wicked creature?"

"Indeed and indeed I have done no such thing. It is not true, Madame Fox, as I can prove. Wait a bit and I will bring witnesses."

So the Duck went out and flew up and down in front of the cave, waiting. Presently along came a Hunter with a gun, who espied the Duck and aimed the weapon at him.

"Don't shoot me," cried the Duck. "What have you against me, O Hunter? I can tell you where to find worthier game. Come with me and I will show you a wicked old Fox who eats innocent birds."

"Very well," said the Hunter, putting up his gun, "show me the place and I will spare you."

The Duck led him softly to the entrance of the cave, and pausing there cried out to the Fox inside, "Come out, Madame Fox, I have brought the witness."

"Let him come in, let him come in!" cried the Fox, for she had grown very hungry indeed and hoped for a double meal.

"No indeed," answered the Duck; "he insists that you must come out." So the Fox crept stealthily to the door, but as soon as she popped out her wicked old head the Hunter was ready for her, and Bang! That was the end of the Fox's pilgrimage.

The Duck also had had enough of being a pilgrim. He went home with the Hunter and became a tame Duck, and lived happily ever after on the pond near the Hunter's house.

THE GROUND-PIGEON

Once upon a time there was a little Malay maiden who lived in the forest with her father and mother and baby sister. They dwelt very happily together, until one day Coora's father decided to clear the ground on the edge of the forest and have a rice plantation, as many of his neighbors were doing.

So one morning early after breakfast he started out with his axe on his shoulder to cut down the trees and make a clearing.

"O Father, let me go with you!" begged Coora. "I do so want to see the plantation grow from the very beginning."

But her father said No, she must stay at home until the trees were felled.

"And after that may I go with you?" asked Coora. And her father promised that it should be so.

The days went by and at last the trees were all felled in the clearing. When Coora heard this she jumped up and down on her little bare brown feet until her anklets tinkled, and cried, "O Father! Now I may go with you to the clearing, may I not? For so you promised."

But again her father shook his head and said, "No, Coora, not yet. You must wait until the fallen timber has been burned off. Then you shall go with your mother and me to the planting of the rice."

Coora was very much disappointed, and the big tears stood in her eyes. But she only said, "Do you promise that I may help plant the rice, really and truly?"

And he called back over his shoulder, "I promise!"

At last the fallen timber was burned away, and the ground was ready for planting. One morning Coora saw her father and mother making ready to go out together. "Oh, where are you going, Father and Mother?" she asked.

"We go to the planting of the rice," answered her father, slinging a big bag over his shoulder.

"But you promised that I should go with you when that time came?" cried Coora wistfully. "Please, please may I not be your little helper?"

"No, no, Coora," answered her mother impatiently. "Do not tease us so. You must stay at home to take care of your little sister. Be a good girl this time, and when the rice is well grown we will all go together and harvest it. That will be great fun!"

"Shall I really go? Do you promise, Mother?" asked poor Coora hopefully, for she felt sure that her mother would not deceive her.

"I promise," said the mother, not looking her in the eyes; and the parents went away through the forest to plant the rice.

Time went by until the rice had grown tall and was ready for the harvest. Now Coora heard her parents talking of the matter, and she was very gay, for now she expected a happy, happy day. She dressed herself and made ready to go to the harvesting, as her parents had promised. But when she joined them, smiling joyfully, they turned upon her frowning and bade her return to the house and take care of everything until their home-coming. Then poor little Coora burst into tears and said, "O my Father and O my Mother, I have obeyed you without a word every time you broke your promise to me. And still you continue to put me off from day to day, when this is the thing I long to do so much that it seems as if my heart would break. Think of it! The clearing has been made, the timber burned, the rice planted and grown, and now it is ready for the harvest. But I have not even seen the place where all this has happened. O Father and Mother, why are you so unkind to me?"

"There, there!" cried her father and mother together, "do not make a fuss over so small a matter. You cannot go to-day; but wait until the rice is gathered and it is time to tread it out. Then we will let you help us, you may be sure. We promise, Coora, that you shall really and truly go."

"You promise!" echoed Coora bitterly. "You have promised me before and nothing came of it." But even while she spoke the unkind parents were gone.

Then Coora fell to weeping most sorely, for she knew that she could not trust the word of her father and mother; and that is a most terrible thing. At last she rose and wiped away the tears and looked about the little cottage where she had been patient through so many disappointments. And she said to herself, "I can bear it no longer. It is not right that I should be made to suffer like this when a little thing would make me so happy. I must see the rice field; I will go to-day."

Coora tidied the cottage, putting everything in its place and making it look as beautiful as she could. Then she took up the little sister who had fallen asleep on the floor, and kissing her tenderly placed her in the hammock which swung from wall to wall of the hut. Lastly Coora took off the golden bracelets and earrings and the tinkling anklets which she wore like other little Malay girls, and left them in a shining heap behind the door. But she kept her necklace about her pretty little neck.

Now Coora had learned a little magic from a witch, just enough magic to serve her turn. She went out and picked two palm leaves which she fastened on her shoulders and changed herself into a bird, a bright, beautiful Ground-Pigeon, with many-colored metallic feathers. But the necklace still made a band about her pretty little neck, as you may see on every Ground-Pigeon to this day.

Coora the Ground-Pigeon fluttered away through the forest until she came to the rice plantation where her parents were at work. She alighted on a dead tree close by them and called out, "Mother, O Mother! I have left my earrings and bracelets behind the door and have put my little sister in the hammock."

Astonished at these words her mother looked up, but saw no one, only a Ground-Pigeon perched on the tree over her head. "Father," she cried to her husband who was at work beside her, "did you not hear Coora's voice just now?"

"Yes, I thought so," answered the father angrily. "The wicked girl must have disobeyed me and have followed us here after all. I will punish her if this is so." They called to her, "Coora, Coora!" until the

forest re 堆 hoed. But no one appeared or answered.

"I will go home and see if she is there," said the mother. "Either I heard Coora speak or there is some magic in the forest." And she hastened back to the cottage. There she found the baby in the hammock and the bracelets and earrings in a shining heap behind the door, as the voice had said, but there was no Coora anywhere. Surprised and anxious, once more the mother ran back to the plantation.

"Coora is gone, husband!" she cried. "It must have been her own voice which we heard just now. Hark! She speaks again!"

Again from the tree they heard a sweet voice calling, "Mother, O Mother, I have left my earrings and bracelets behind the door and my little sister in the hammock. Good-by, Coo-o-o-ra!" As she spoke her own name Coora's voice warbled and crooned into the soft coo of a Ground-Pigeon's note, and her parents glancing up saw that this bird must be their child, their Coora, magically changed.

"Let us cut down the tree and catch the wicked girl!" cried the father. And seizing his axe he chopped away lustily until the tree fell with a crash. But even at that moment the Pigeon fluttered away to another tree, crooning again the soft syllables which she has spoken ever since, "Coo-ra, coo-ra, coo!"

From tree to tree about the rice plantation the distracted parents pursued the Pigeon; but it was in vain to try to capture her. Ever she escaped them when they seemed about to lay hands upon her soft feathers. After following her flight for many miles they were obliged to return home, sad and sorry and repentant. For they knew now that it was their own unkindness and their broken promises which had driven their daughter away from the cottage, never to return.

The beautiful Ground-Pigeon still lingers near the rice plantations which she had so longed to visit. Still she plaintively calls her name, and still she wears the necklace about her pretty little neck. And the little Malay maidens love her very dearly because she was once a girl like them.

SISTER HEN AND THE CROCODILE

The Crocodile is one of the hungriest bodies that ever lived. When he is looking for a dinner he will eat almost anything that comes within reach. Sometimes the greedy fellow swallows great stones and chunks of wood, in his hurry mistaking them for something more digestible. And when he is smacking his great jaws over his food he makes such a greedy, terrible noise that the other animals steal away nervously and hide until it shall be Master Crocodile's sleepy-time. He is too lazy to waddle in search of a dinner far from the river where he lives. But any animal or even a man-swimmer had best be careful how he ventures into the water near the Crocodile's haunts. For what seems to be a greenish-brown, knobby log of wood floating on the water, has little bright eyes which are on the lookout for anything which moves. And below the water two great jaws are ready to open and swallow in the prey of Mr. Hungry-Mouth.

But no matter how hungry the Crocodile may be, he will not touch the Hen, even if she should venture into his very jaws; at least, that is what the Black Men of the Congo River will tell you. And surely, as they are the nearest neighbors of the big reptile they ought to know if any one does. Now this is the story which they tell to explain why the Crocodile will not eat the Hen.

Once upon a time there was a Hen, a common, plump, clucky mother Hen, who used every day to go down to the river and pick up bits of food on the moist banks, where luscious insects were many. She did not know that this Congo River was the home of the Crocodile, the biggest, fiercest, scaliest, hungriest Crocodile in all Africa. But one day when she went down to the water as usual she hopped out onto what looked like a mossy log, saying to herself:--

"Aha! This is a fine old timber-house. It is full of juicy bugs, I know. I shall have a great feast!"

Tap-tap! Pick-pick! The Hen began to scratch and peck upon the rough bark of the log, but Oh dear me! suddenly she began to feel very seasick. The log was rolling over! The log was teetering up on end like a boat in a storm! And before she knew what was really happening the poor Hen found herself floundering in the water in the very jaws of the terrible Crocodile.

"Ha, ha!" cried the Crocodile in his harsh voice. "You took me for a log, just as the other silly creatures do. But I am no log, Mrs. Hen, as you shall soon see. I am Hungry Crocodile, and you will make the fifth dinner which I have had this evening."

The Hen was frightened almost to death, but she kept her presence of mind and gasped frantically as she saw the great jaws opening to swallow her:--

"O Brother, don't!"

Now the Crocodile was so surprised at hearing the Hen call him Brother that he kept his jaws wide open and forgot to swallow his dinner. He kept them open for some time, gaping foolishly, wondering what the Hen could mean, and how he could possibly be her brother. And by the time he had remembered how hungry he was, there was nothing for him to eat. For the Hen had skipped away just as fast as her feet would take her.

"Pouf!" snorted the Crocodile. "Her brother, indeed! I am not her brother, and she knows it very well. What a fool I was to be caught by such a word! Just wait till I catch her again and we will see. I will brother her!" And he swam sulkily away to hide his mortification in the Congo mud, with only the end of his long nose poking out as a ventilator for his breathing.

Now, though the Hen had had so narrow an escape, it had not sufficiently taught her a lesson. A few days afterwards once more she went down to the river, for she could not resist the temptation of the bug-dinner which she knew she should find there. But she kept her eyes open sharply for any greeny log which might be floating on the water, saying to herself, "Old Hungry-Mouth shall not catch me napping this time. I know his wicked tricks!"

But this time the Crocodile was not floating on the water like a greeny log. He was lying still as still, sunning himself on the river bank behind some tall reeds. Mrs. Hen came trotting down to the water, a plump and tempting sight, cocking her head knowingly on one side as she spied a real log floating out beyond, which she took to be her enemy. And as she scratched in the soft mud, chuckling to think how sly she was, with a rush and a rustle down pounced the

Crocodile upon her, and once more, before she knew it, she found herself in the horrid gateway of his jaws, threatened by the double rows of long, white teeth.

"Oho!" snapped the Crocodile. "You shall not escape me this time. I am a log, am I? Look at me again, Mrs. Hen. Am I a log?" And he came at her to swallow her at once.

But again the Hen squawked, "O Brother, don't!"

Again the Crocodile paused, thunderstruck by this extraordinary word. "Oh, bother the Hen!" he cried, "what can she mean, really? How can I be her brother? She lives in a town on the land, and I live in my kingdom of mud and water. How could two creatures possibly be more unlike? How"--but while he had been thinking of these hows, once more the Hen had managed to escape, and was pelting back to her barnyard as fast as she could go.

Then indeed the Crocodile was angry. He determined to go and see Nzambi, the wise witch princess, about the matter. She would tell him what it all meant. But it was a long journey to her palace and he was awkward and slow in traveling upon land. Before he had gone very far he was tired and out of breath, and stopped to rest under a banana tree.

As he lay panting in the shade he saw his friend Mbambi, the great Lizard, hurrying past through the jungle.

"Oh, Mbambi!" cried old Hungry-Mouth, "stop a moment. I want to speak with you. I am in great trouble."

So the Lizard drew near, wagging her head wisely, for it pleased her to be consulted by the big Crocodile. "What can it be, dear friend, that is troubling you this day?" she said amiably. "Surely, no one would be so rude or rash as to offend the King of Congo River. But tell me your trouble and perhaps I can advise you."

"Listen to me, then," said the Crocodile. "Almost every day a nice fat Hen,--Oh, Mbambi! so delightfully fat and tempting!--comes to my river to feed. Well, why don't I make her my dinner? you ask. Now hearken: each time, just as I am about to catch her and carry her to my home she startles me by calling me 'Brother.' Did you ever hear of anything so maddening? Twice I have let her escape because of the word. But I can stand it no longer, and I am on the way to Princess Nzambi to hold a palaver about it." (By "palaver" the slangy Crocodile meant a long, serious talk.)

"Silly idiot!" cried the Mbambi, not very politely. "Do nothing of the kind. You will only get the worst of the palaver and show your ignorance before the wise Nzambi. Now listen to me. Don't you know, dear Crocodile, that the Duck lives on the water, though she is neither a fish nor a reptile? And the Duck lays eggs. The Turtle does the same, though she is no bird. The Hen lays eggs, just as I do; and I am Mbambi, the great Lizard. As for you, dear old Hungry-Mouth, you know that at this moment"--here she whispered discreetly, looking around to see that no one was listening,--"at this moment in a snug nest dug out of the sand on the banks of the Congo, Mrs. Crocodile has covered with leaves to hide them from your enemies sixty smooth white eggs. And in a few weeks out of these will scamper sixty little wiggly Crocodiles, your dear, homely, scaly, hungry-mouthed children. Yes, we all lay eggs, my silly friend, and so in a sense we are all brothers, as the Hen has said."

"Sh!" whispered the Crocodile, nervously. "Don't mention those eggs of mine, I beg of you. Some one might overhear. What you say is undoubtedly true," he added pensively, after thinking a few moments. "Then I suppose I must give up my tempting dinner of Hen. I cannot eat my Sister, can I?"

"Of course you cannot," said the Mbambi, as he rustled away through the jungle. "We can't have everything we want in this world."

"No, I see we cannot," sighed the Crocodile, as he waddled back towards the banks of the Congo. Now in the same old spot he found the Hen, who had been improving his absence by greedily stuffing herself on beetle-bugs, flies, and mosquitoes until she was so fat that she could not run away at the Crocodile's approach. She could only stand and squawk feebly, fluttering her ridiculous wings.

But the Crocodile only said, "Good evening, Sister," very politely, and passing her by with a wag of his enormous tail sank with a plop into the waters of the Congo.

And ever since that time the Hen has eaten her dinner in tranquil peace, undisturbed by the sight of floating log or basking shape of knobby green. For she knows that old Hungry-Mouth will not eat his Sister, the Hen.

THE THRUSH AND THE CUCKOO

In the wonderful days of old it is said that Christ and Saint Peter went together upon a journey. It was a beautiful day in March, and the earth was just beginning to put on her summer gorgeousness. As the two travelers were passing near a great forest they spied a Thrush sitting on a tree singing and singing as hard as he could. And he cocked his head as if he was very proud of something.

Saint Peter stopped at the foot of the tree and said, "I wish you a good day, Thrush!"

"I have no time to thank you," chirped the Thrush pertly.

"Why not, pretty Thrush?" asked Saint Peter in surprise. "You have all the time in the world and nothing to do but sing."

"You mistake," cried the Thrush. "I am making the summer! It is I, I, I who make the green grass grow and the flowers bud. Look, how even now the world is growing beautiful in answer to my song." And the conceited little bird continued to warble as hard as he could,--

"To-day I shall marry, I and no other! To-morrow my brother."

Christ and Saint Peter looked at each other and smiled, then went upon their way without another word, leaving the Thrush to continue his task of making the summer.

This was in the morning. But before midday the clouds gathered and the sky darkened, and at noon a cold rain began to drip. The poor Thrush ceased his jubilant song and began to shiver in the March wind. By night the snow was felling thick and fast, and where there had been a green carpet on the earth was now spread a coverlet of snowy white. Shivering and like to die of cold the Thrush took refuge under the tree in the moss and dead leaves. He thought no more of his marriage, nor of his brother's, but only of the danger which threatened him, and of the discomfort.

The next morning Christ and Saint Peter, plodding through the snow-drifts, came upon him again, and Saint Peter said as before, "I wish you good day, Thrush."

"Thank you," answered the Thrush humbly, and his voice was shaky with cold and sorrow.

"What do you here on the cold ground, O Thrush-who-make-the-summer, and why are you so sad?" asked Saint Peter. And the

Thrush piped feebly,--

"To-day I must die, I and no other! To-morrow my brother."

"O foolish little bird," said Saint Peter. "You boasted that you made the summer. But see! The Lord's will has sent us back to the middle of winter, to punish your boasting. You shall not die, he will send the sun again to warm you. But hereafter beware how you take too much credit for your little efforts."

Since that time March has ever been a treacherous and a changeful month. Then the Thrush thinks not of marriage, but of his lesson learned in past days, and wraps himself in his warmest feathers, waiting for the Lord's will to be done. He is no longer boastful in his song, but sings it humbly and sweetly to the Lord's glory, thanking him for the summer which his goodness sends every year to happy bird and beast and child of man.

* * * * *

Now after this adventure with the Thrush, Christ and Saint Peter went upon their journey for many miles. At last, weary and hungry, they passed a Baker's shop. From the window came the smell of new warm bread baking in the oven, and Christ sent Saint Peter to ask the Baker for a loaf. But the Baker, who was a stingy fellow, refused.

"Go away with you!" he cried. "I give no bread to lazy beggars!"

"I ask it for my Master, who has traveled many miles and is most faint and weary," said Saint Peter. But the Baker frowned and shook his head, then strode into the inner shop, banging the door after him.

The Baker's wife and six daughters were standing at one side when these things happened, and they heard all that took place. They were generous and kind-hearted bodies, and tears stood in their eyes at the Baker's rough words. As soon as he had gone out they wrapped up the loaf and gave it stealthily to Saint Peter saying,--

"Take the loaf for your Master, good man, and may he be refreshed by it."

Saint Peter thanked and blessed them and took the loaf to Christ. And for their charity the Lord set these good women in the sky as the Seven Stars,--you may see them to this day shining in love upon the sleeping world. But the wicked Baker he changed into a Cuckoo; and as long as he sings his dreary song, "Coo-coo! Coo-coo!" in the spring, so long the Seven Stars are visible in the heaven, so folk say.

THE OWL AND THE MOON

When the moon is round and full, if you look very carefully at the golden disk you can see in shadowy outline the profile of a beautiful lady. She is leaning forward as if looking down upon our earth, and there is a little smile upon her sweet lips. This fair dame is Putri Balan, the Princess of the Moon, and she smiles because she remembers how once upon a time she cheated old Mr. Owl, her tiresome lover.

Putri Balan, so they tell you in Malay, was always very, very beautiful, as we see her now. Like all the Malay women, Putri Balan loved to chew the spicy betel-nut which turns one's lips a bright scarlet. It is better, so they say, than any kind of candy, and it is considered much nicer and more respectable than chewing-gum. So Putri Balan was not unladylike, although she chewed her betel-nut all night long.

Now, ever since the day when Mr. Owl carelessly let the naughty little Wren escape from prison, the shamed and sorry old fellow had never dared to show his face abroad in daylight. Gradually his eyes grew blurred and blinky, till now he could not see anything by day, even if he were to try.

So it happens that there are many delightful things about which old Mr. Owl does not know,--things which take place while the beautiful sun is shining. But also there are marvelous sights, unknown to early-sleeping birds, which he enjoys all by himself. For at night his queer eyes are wonderfully strong and bright. All day long he sits in his hollow tree, but when the other feathered folk are drowsing upon their roosts, or are snugly rolled up in their little nests, with their heads tucked under their downy wings, old Mr. Owl puts on his round spectacles and goes a-prowling up and down the world through the woods and meadows (like Haroun-al-Rashid in the streets of Bagdad), spying all sorts of queer doings.

And this is how old Mr. Owl happened to see the fair Princess Putri Balan, smiling down from her moon upon the sleeping world of birds who had never seen her and never would see her in all her loveliness.

How beautiful she was! How bright and wonderful! Old Mr. Owl stared up in wide-eyed astonishment, and then and there fell in love with her, and resolved to ask her to be his wife.

Cramming on his spectacles more tightly and ruffling the feathers about his neck, he flew up and up and up, as high as ever he dared to go, until he was within hailing distance of the moon. Then he called out in his softest tones,--which were harsh enough to any ears,--

"O fair Moon-Maiden, O beautiful Princess, will you marry me? For I love you very dearly."

The Princess Putri Balan stopped chewing her betel-nut for a moment and looked down to see what daring creature might thus be addressing her. Soon she spied Mr. Owl with his goggle-eyes looking up at her adoringly. He was such a ridiculous old creature, and his spectacles glinted so queerly in the moonlight, that Putri Balan began to laugh and answered him not at all. She laughed so hard that she almost swallowed her betel-nut, which might have been a serious matter.

Mr. Owl continued to stare, for he saw nothing funny in the situation. Again he repeated in his hoarse voice, "O fair Moon-Maiden, O beautiful Princess, will you marry me? For I love you very dearly."

Again the Princess laughed, for she thought it a tremendous joke; and again she nearly choked. Mr. Owl waited, but she made him no other answer. However, he was a persistent lover. All night long he went on asking the same question, over and over again, until the Princess Putri Balan was quite worn out trying not to choke with laughter while she chewed the betel-nut. At last she said impatiently,--

"O Mr. Goggle-Eyes! Do give me a moment's peace! You make me laugh so that I cannot chew my betel-nut. Yes, I will say yes, if you will only leave me to finish my betel-nut undisturbed. I will marry you. But you must go away until I have quite done."

Then Mr. Owl was filled with joy. "Thanks, thanks, O most gracious lady!" he said. "I will go away and leave you to finish your betel-nut undisturbed. But I shall come again to-morrow night, and by that time you will have done with it, and then you will be mine!"

Mr. Owl flew back to his home in the hollow tree, for it was almost morning, and already he was growing so blind that he could hardly find the way. But the Princess Putri Balan went on chewing the betel-nut, and to herself she said,--

[Illustration: _Putri Balan began to laugh_]

"How am I to rid myself of this bore? I cannot chew this little betel-nut forever; there must be an end to it before long. Mr. Owl will certainly come again to-morrow night, and then, according to my promise, I must become his wife. I cannot marry old Goggle-Eyes. Oh dear! What shall I do?"

As she chewed her betel-nut the Princess Putri Balan hit upon a plan. She would manage to cheat old Mr. Owl after all. She would never finish the betel-nut! She took the little bit that remained,--and it was a dangerously little bit, for the Princess had been chewing all night long, except when she was laughing,--and reaching out from the moon she tossed it down, down, down upon the earth. At the same time she said a magic moon-charm: and when the bit of betel-nut reached the earth, it became a little bird,--the same which the Malay people call the Honey Bird, with brilliant, beautiful plumage. And the Princess Putri Balan cried out to it from her golden house,--

"Fly away, pretty little bright bird! Fly as far and as fast as ever you can, and keep out of Mr. Owl's way. For it is you who must save me from becoming his unhappy wife."

So the Honey Bird flew away, a brilliant streak, through the Malay woods, and hid himself in a little nest.

When night came out stole Mr. Owl, with his spectacles in place, and up he flew to his Princess, whom he now hoped to call his very own.

"Good evening, my beautiful Princess!" he cried. "Have you finished your betel-nut at last, and are you ready to keep your promise?"

But the Princess Putri Balan looked down at him, pretending to be sad, though there was a twinkle in her beautiful eye; and she said,--

"Alas! Mr. Owl, a dreadful thing has happened. I lost my betel-nut, before it was quite finished. It fell down, down, down, until I think it reached the earth. And I cannot marry you, according to my promise, until it is finished."

"Then it must be found!" cried Mr. Owl. "I will find it. My eyes are sharp at night and nothing escapes them. Shine kindly on me, Princess, and I will find the betel-nut for you, and you shall yet be mine."

"Go then, Mr. Owl," said the Princess, smiling to herself. "Go and look for the betel-nut which I must finish before I marry you. Search carefully and you may find it soon."

Poor Mr. Owl searched carefully, but he could not find the bit of betel-nut. Of course he could not find it, when it had changed and flown away as a beautiful, many-colored bird! All that night he sought, till the sun sent him blinking to his tree. And all the next night he sought, and the next, and the next. And he kept on seeking for days and months and years, while the Princess Putri Balan smiled down upon him and was happy at heart because of her clever scheme.

Old Mr. Owl never found out the trick, nor suspected the innocent little Honey Bird, whom indeed he scarcely ever saw, because it was a sunset-sleeping bird, while he was a wistful, lonely, sad night-prowler. Up and down, up and down the world he goes, still looking for the betel-nut of the Princess Putri Balan, which he will never find. And as he flies in the moonlight he glances ever longingly at the beautiful lady in the moon, and sobs "Hoo-hoo! Hoo-hoo!" in grief and despair. For after all these centuries he begins to fear that she will never be his wife.

THE TUFTED CAP

One dark night Master Owl left his hollow tree and went prowling about the world as usual upon his hopeless hunt for the Princess's betel-nut. As soon as he was out of hearing a long, lean, hungry Rat crept to the house and stole the dainties which the lonely old bachelor had stored away for the morrow's dinner. The thief dragged them away to his own hole and had a splendid feast with his wife and little ones. But the Owl returned sooner than the Rat had expected, and by the crumbs which he had dropped upon the way tracked him to the hole.

"Come out, thief!" cried the Owl, "or I will surely kill you. Come out and return to me my morrow's dinner." The Rat trembled with fear at these threatening words.

"Alas!" he squeaked, "I cannot do that, for already the dinner is eaten. My wife and hungry little ones have eaten it. Pity us, for we were starving!"

"Bah!" screamed the Owl, "I care little for that. It is for my dinner alone that I care. Since you have eaten it you shall certainly die," and he began to scratch fiercely at the mouth of the hole. The Rat trembled more than ever. But suddenly he had an idea which made his whiskers twitch.

"Hold!" he cried. "Dear, good Master Owl, permit me to live and I will give you something which is worth many dinners, something that men-creatures value very highly, and which with great labor and pain I brought away from one of their dens."

"Umph!" grumbled the Owl. "Let us see what it is."

The Rat crawled timidly out of his hole with the peace-offering; and what do you think it was? Why, a gimlet! Just a plain, ordinary, well-sharpened gimlet for boring holes.

"Hoo!" cried the Owl. "I don't think much of that. What is it good for?" Now the Rat had not the faintest idea as to what the gimlet really was, but he had another idea instead.

"That? Why--that--oh, that! That is a very valuable thing. It is able to give you the keenest delight. I will show you how it works. But you must do just as I say, or it will be of no use."

"Hoo!" cried the Owl. "Continue with the directions."

"Well, first you must stick the thing point upwards in the ground at the foot of this tree."

"Very good," said the Owl, doing as was suggested, and waiting expectantly for the next move.

"Now you must mount to the top of the tree and slide down the trunk," said the Rat solemnly. Old Master Owl was certainly very far from wise that night, for he obeyed the Rat's word without a suspicion. He flew to the top of the tree, and then, sitting back and giving a warning cry of "Hoo-hoo!" coasted down the trunk with the speed of lightning. But midway down he struck a knot in the tree and rolled heels over head. And when he reached the ground of course he landed fast upon the sharp point of the gimlet, just as the Rat had planned.

With bloody head, and hooting with pain, the Owl started off in pursuit of the Rat, resolved this time to kill him without fail. The Rat was nimble, and his fear added to his speed, but at last the Owl caught him. Ruffled and ferocious, the great bird was about to tear him in pieces, when the Rat once more begged his life.

"It was only a joke," he cried. "Only a silly joke. Spare me this once, dear Master Owl, and I will give you something that you really need. Look at your bleeding head. You cannot go about the world with that exposed. Spare my life, and I will give you a lovely cap of tufted feathers to hide the bite of the wicked sharp-thing-made-by-man. Pray, let me go, dear Master Owl."

The Owl considered for a moment, and then decided to accept the bargain. For he thought of Putri Balan, the Princess of the Moon, and knew that he should lose his last chance to win her if she happened to see him with this ridiculous wound in his head.

So the Rat gave him a nice cap of tufted feathers, which he wears to this day; and the Owl let the thief go free. But after that there was a coolness between them, as you may well imagine.

THE GOOD HUNTER

Once upon a time there was an Indian who was a famous hunter. But he did not hunt for fun; he took no pleasure in killing the little wild creatures, birds and beasts and fishes, and did so only when it was necessary for him to have food or skins for his clothing. He was a very kind and generous man, and loved all the wood-creatures dearly, often feeding them from his own larder, and protecting them from their enemies. So the animals and birds loved him as their best friend, and he was known as the Good Hunter.

The Good Hunter was very brave, and often went to war with the fierce savages who were the enemies of his tribe. One sad day he set forth with a war party, and they had a terrible battle, in which the

Good Hunter was slain, and his enemies took away his scalp, leaving him lying dead in the forest.

The Good Hunter had not remained long cold and lifeless in the shadowy stillness, when the Fox came trotting through the woods. "Alack and alas!" cried the Fox, spying the body stretched on the leaves. "Here is our dear friend, the Good Hunter, slain! Alack and alas! what shall we do now that our dear friend and protector is gone?"

The Fox ran out into the forest crying the death lament, which was the signal to all the beasts that something most sorrowful had happened. Soon they came flocking to the spot, all the animals of the forest. By hundreds they came, and surrounding the body of their friend raised the most doleful howls. For, though they rubbed him with their warm noses, and licked him with their warm tongues, and nestled against him with their warm fur, they could not bring him back to warm life.

They called upon Brother Bear to speak and tell them what to do; for he was the nearest relative to man. The Bear sat up on his haunches and spoke to the sad assembly with tears in his eyes, begging each animal to look carefully through his medicine-box and see whether there might not be some balm which would restore the Good Hunter to life. Then each animal looked carefully through his medicine-box of herbs and healing roots, bark and magic leaves, and they tried every remedy that they knew. But nothing brought the color to their friend's pale cheeks, nor light into his eyes. He who had helped them so often was helpless now, and they could not aid him. Again the kind beasts sank back on their haunches and raised a mighty howl, a requiem for the dead.

Wild and piercing and long-drawn, the sound swept through the forest, such a sound of sorrow as had never been heard before. The

Oriole, who was flying overhead, heard and was surprised. Soon his brightness came flashing down through the leafy boughs like a ray of sunlight into the gloom and darkness of the forest.

"What has happened, O four-footed friends," he asked, "that you mourn so mightily?" Then they showed him the body of the Good Hunter lying in the midst of their sad company, and the Oriole joined his voice of sorrow to theirs.

"O friend of the birds," he cried, "is there no bird who can aid you now, you who have fed us so many times from the door of your generous wigwam? I will call all the feathered tribes, and we will do our best."

So the Oriole went forth and summoned the birds to the forest council. There was a great flapping of wings, a great twittering and chirping, questioning and exclamation when the birds assembled to hear the sad news. Every one was there, from the tiny Humming Bird to the great Eagle of the Iroquois, who left his lonely eyrie to pay his respects to the Good Hunter's memory. The poor little birds tried everything in their power to bring back to life their dear friend. With beak and claw and tender wing they strove, but all their efforts were in vain. Their Good Hunter was dead, and his scalp was gone.

Then the great Eagle, whose head was white with years of wisdom and experience, spoke to the despairing assemblage of creatures. From his lofty perch above the world the Eagle had looked down upon centuries of change and decay. He knew every force of nature and all the strange things of life. The hoary-headed sage said that the Good Hunter could not be restored until his scalp was found. Then all the animals clamored that they might be allowed to go and seek for the missing scalp. But to the Fox was given this honor, because he had first found the body of the Good Hunter in the forest. The Fox set out upon his search, in his foxy way. He visited every henroost and every bird's-nest, but no scalp did he find. "Of course not!" screamed the birds when he returned from his fruitless quest, "Of course no bird has taken the Good Hunter's scalp. You should have known better than that, Master Fox."

So the next time a bird was sent upon the search. The Pigeon Hawk went forth, confident that she should be successful. But she was in such a hurry and flew so fast that she saw nothing, and she too returned without that for which she sought. Then the White Heron begged that he might be allowed to try. "For," said he, "you all know how slowly I fly, and how careful I am to see everything."

"Yes, especially if it be something good to eat," chirped the saucy Jay, "do not trust him, birds, he is too greedy."

Yet the Heron was allowed to go. He flapped away, slowly and sedately, and the Council sat down to await his return. But the Heron had not gone far when he came to a field of luscious wild beans; and he stopped to take a mouthful or two. He ate, and he ate, and he ate, the greedy fellow! until he could eat no more. And then he was sleepy, so that he slept and slept and slept. And when he awoke he was so hungry that he fell to eating again, while the Council waited and wondered and waited. At last they grew impatient and began to suspect that the Jay had been right, which was indeed the case. They decided to wait no longer for the Heron, who did not return. Then the Crow stepped forward and said, "Let me go, I pray you, for I think I know where the scalp may be found; not in the nest of a bird, not in the den of any animal, not in the watery haunt of a fish. For all the creatures of earth, air, and water are friends of the Good Hunter. It is men who are most cruel to men: therefore in the tents of men must we look for the missing scalp. Let me go to seek it there, for men are used to see me flying near and will not suspect why I come."

The Crow flew forth upon his errand, and before long came to the wigwam where lived the warrior who had slain the Good Hunter. And sure enough, there, outside the tent, was the scalp of the Good Hunter, stretched on a pole to dry. The Crow flew near, and the warrior saw him, but thought nothing of it, for he was used to seeing crows about the camp. Presently when no one was looking the skillful thief managed to steal the scalp, and away he flew with it to the Council in the forest. Great was the rejoicing of the birds and beasts when they saw that the Crow had been successful, and they said more kind things to him than he had heard for many moons. At once they put the scalp upon the Good Hunter's head, but it had grown so dry in the smoke of the warrior's wigwam that it would not fit. Here was a new trouble. What was to be done to make the scalp soft and flexible once more? The animals did their best, but their efforts were of no avail.

Once more the great Eagle came forward and bade them listen.

"My children," he said, "my wings are never furled. Night and day for hundreds of years the dews of heaven have been collecting upon my back as I sit on my throne above the clouds. Perhaps this dew may have a healing power such as no earthly fountain holds. We will see."

Gravely the Eagle plucked a long feather, and dipping it in the dew which moistened his plumage, applied it to the stiffened scalp. Immediately it became soft, and could be fitted to the head of the Good Hunter closely as when it had first grown there. The birds and animals hurried away and brought leaves and flowers, bark and berries and roots, which they made into a mighty healing balsam to bathe the poor head which had been so cruelly treated. And presently great was their joy to see a soft color come into the pale cheeks of the Good Hunter, and light into his eyes. He breathed, he stirred, he sat up and looked around him in surprise.

"Where am I? What has happened?" he asked.

"You slept and your friends have wakened you," said the great Eagle tenderly. "Stand up, Good Hunter, that they may see you walk once more."

The Good Hunter stood up and walked, rather unsteadily at first, back to his own wigwam, followed by a great company of happy forest creatures, who made the sky ring with their noises of rejoicing. And long, long after that, the Good Hunter lived to love and protect them.

THE COURTSHIP OF MR. STORK AND MISS HERON

This is a very good story to read at night just before going to sleep. And if you ask why, I must only tell you that you will find out before you reach the end of the tale.

* * * * *

There was once a Heron, a pretty, long-legged, slender lady Heron, who lived in the mushy-squshy, wady-shady swamp. The lady Heron lived in her swamp all alone, earning her living by catching little fish; and she was very happy, never dreaming that she was lonesome, for no one had told her what lonesome was. She loved to go wading in the cool waters; she loved to catch the little fish who swam by unsuspectingly while she stood still upon one leg pretending to think about something a thousand miles away. And she loved to look at her slender, long-legged blue reflection in the water; for the lady Heron was just a little bit vain.

Now one day Mr. Stork came flying over the mushy-squshy, wady-shady swamp where the Heron lived, and he too saw the reflection in the water. And he said to himself, "My! How pretty she is! I wonder I never noticed her before. And how lonesome she must be there all by herself in such a nasty, moist, mushy-squshy old swamp! I will invite her to come and share my nice, warm, dry nest on the chimney-top. For to tell the truth, I am growing lonely up there all by myself. Why should we not make a match of it, we two long-legged creatures?"

Mr. Stork went home to his house, which he set prettily in order: for he never dreamed but that the lady Heron would accept his offer at the very first croak. He preened his feathers and made himself as lovely as he could, and forthwith off he flew with his long legs dangling, straight to the wady-shady swamp where Miss Heron was standing on one leg waiting for her supper to get itself caught.

"Ahem!" croaked Mr. Stork, waving his wing politely. "Good evening, Miss Heron. Fine weather we are having, eh? But how horribly moist it is down here! I should think that your nice straight legs would grow crooked with rheumatism. Now I have a comfortable, dry house on the roof."

"Pouf!" grunted Miss Heron disdainfully.

But Mr. Stork pretended not to hear, and went on with his remarks,--"a nice dry house which I should be glad to have you share with me. Come, Miss Heron! Here I am a lonely old bachelor, and here are you a lonely old maid"--

"Lonely old maid, indeed!" screamed the Heron interrupting him. "I don't know what it is to be lonely. Go along with you!" and she splashed water on him with her wings, she was so indignant.

Poor Mr. Stork felt very crestfallen at this reception of his well-meaning invitation. He turned about and stalked away towards his nest upon the roof, without so much as saying good-by to the lady.

But no sooner was he out of sight than Miss Heron began to think. He had said that she was lonely; was she lonely? Well, perhaps he ought to know better than she, for he was a very wise bird. Perhaps she was lonely, now that she came to think of it. However, there was no reason why she should go to live in that stupid, dry, old nest on the house-top. Why could he not come to dwell in her lovely, mushy-squshy, wady-shady swamp? That would be very pleasant, for he was a good sort of fellow with nice long legs; and there were fish enough in the water for two. Besides, he could then do the fishing for the family; and, moreover, there would then be two to admire her reflection in the water. Yes; her mind was made up. She would invite him. She glanced down at her reflection and settled some of the feathers which her fit of temper had ruffled out of order. Then off she started in pursuit of Mr. Stork.

Mr. Stork had not gone very far, for a sad, rejected lover is a dawdling creature. And so she came up with him long before he was in sight of his nest.

"Good evening, Mr. Stork," said the lady nervously. "I--I have been thinking over what you said to me just now, and I have concluded that perhaps I was a bit hasty. To tell you the truth, sir, I am a trifle lonely, now that you suggest the thought to me. And it would be very agreeable to have pleasant company. I am ready, sir, to agree to your proposal. But of course I cannot think of changing my abode. My swamp is the most beautiful home that a maiden ever knew, and I could not give it up for any one. As for your ugly old nest on the chimney-top, bah! I cannot endure the idea with patience."

Mr. Stork was gradually stiffening into an angry attitude, but she did not notice. "Now you can come and live in my swamp," Miss Heron went on warmly, "and you will be very welcome to catch fish for me, and to look in my mirror. It will be very nice indeed!"

"Nice!" croaked the Stork, "I should say as much! What can you be thinking of, Miss? I to give up my comfortable home on the house-top, close by the warm chimney, and go to live in that disgusting mushy-squshy bog of yours! Ha-ha! That is really too ridiculous! I bid you good morning." And with an elaborate bow he turned his back and flew away.

Miss Heron flounced back to her swamp, mortified because she had left it to propose terms to so ungallant a fellow. But hardly had she begun her tardy supper when once more Mr. Stork's shadow darkened the mirror before her, and once more she heard his apologetic croak.

"Ahem, ahem!" he began. "I hope I find you well, Miss Heron? I have been--ha hum!--considering your last most condescending words, and I find that I have been hasty. You are so good as to express a belief that I should make a pleasant companion. So I should! so I should! And as for you," he bowed gallantly, "one can readily imagine the charm of your society. Come, then, Miss Heron, why should we not make a happy couple, if we can only arrange this one little foolish matter? Be my wife: come live with me in my lovely nest."

But at this word Miss Heron uttered a little scream and cried, "Be off with you, you villain! Leave my premises instantly!" and she waved her wings so fiercely that once more Mr. Stork took to his and flapped away to his home.

Now when he had gone Miss Heron found that she had been bad-tempered, and she thought how pleasantly they might have arranged the matter if only she had been more moderate. So she spread her beautiful blue wings and flew to the housetop where Mr. Stork lived, and, perching on the chimney, she said,--

"Oh, Mr. Stork, I was bad-tempered and impolite, and I beg your pardon. Let us be friends once more. Leave this hot old stupid house-top and come live in my cool, moist, wady-shady swamp, and I will be your very loving little wife."

But the Stork arose in his nest, flapping his wings crossly, and cried, "Be off, you baggage! Don't come here to insult my beautiful house. Be off, I say, to your mushy-squshy, rheumaticky bog. I want no more of you!"

So the Heron flew back disconsolately to the watery swamp, where she began to feel very lonely indeed. And the Stork, too, began to feel very lonely indeed; and he was sorry that he had been rude to a lady. Presently, once more he came flapping to the mushy-squshy marsh, where he found Miss Heron just ready to go to sleep.

"Oh, dear Miss Heron!" he cried. "I made a great mistake, and said things for which I am truly sorry. Do come to be my loving wife, as you promised, and we will live happily ever after on the chimney-top, far above the other birds. And I will never be cross again."

But the Heron answered, "Away with you! I want to go to sleep. I am tired of your croaking voice. Leave me alone!" So the Stork flew away in a huff.

But the Heron could not sleep, she was so lonely. So she rose, and, flying through the still night air, came again to the Stork's high-built nest.

"Come, Storkie dear," she said in her sweetest tone, "come home to your dear wife's house in the wady-shady, mushy-squshy marsh, and I will be good."

But the Stork pretended to be asleep, and only snored in reply. So the Heron flew home in a huff. But the Stork could not truly sleep, he was so lonely. So he rose, and, flying through the still night air, came again to the Heron's home in the marsh.

"Come, my dear," he said. "Come home to your dear husband's house, and I will be good."

But the Heron made no answer, pretending to be asleep. So the Stork flew home in a huff. But the Heron could not truly sleep, she was so lonely. So she rose at break of day, and, flying through the cool morning air, came again to the Stork's nest.

"Come, Storkie dear," she said, "come home to your dear wife's house, and I will be good."

But the Stork did not answer, he was so angry. So the Heron flew home in a huff.

* * * * *

And if you are not asleep when you get as far as this, you may go on with the story by yourself, perfectly well. You may go on just as long as you can keep awake. For the tale has no end, no end at all. It is still going on to this very day. The Stork still lives lonely on his house-top, and the Heron still lives lonely in her marsh, growing lonelier and lonelier, both of them. But because they have no tact, they are never able to agree to the same thing at the same time. And they keep flying back and forth, saying the same things over, and over, and over, and over....

THE PHOENIX

On the top of a palm tree, in an oasis of the Arabian desert, sat the Phoenix, glowering moodily upon the world below. He was alone, quite alone, in his old age, as he had been alone in his youth, and in his middle years; for the Phoenix has neither mate nor children, and there is never but one of his kind upon the earth.

Once he had been proud of his solitariness and of his unusual beauty, which caused such wonder when he went abroad. But now he was old and weak and weary, and he was lonely, oh! so lonely! He had lived too long, he thought.

For years and years and years, afar and apart, he had watched the coming and going of things in the world. He had seen the other birds created, and had watched them undergo strange changes in form and color until they became as they are to-day. He had seen the hundred bright eyes of Argus, the watchman, set in the Peacock's tail. He had seen the flaming heart of the volcano tamed and quieted until it became the flaming little Humming-Bird. He had seen the Crow turn black and the Goldfinch become a gaudy bird, and he knew how and why all these things had come to pass. For centuries, how many he knew not, he had watched the birds hatch out of their little eggs, flutter their feeble little wings, fly away to build nests for their little mates, and finally die and disappear as birds do, leaving no trace behind.

But the Phoenix did not die. He was of different clay from these ordinary feathered creatures. He was the glorious bird of the Sun, the only one, the gold-and-crimson one, who when he went abroad filled all creatures with awe of his beauty and wisdom and mystery, so that they dared not come near, but followed him afar off, hushing their song and adoring silently. The Phoenix fed not on flowers or fruit or disgusting insect-fry, but on precious frankincense and myrrh and odoriferous gums. And the Sun himself loved to caress his plumage of gold and crimson.

As for men, they also had adored him in time past, and had built temples in his honor. They also were puny mortals, scarcely longer of life than the birds themselves. The Phoenix had seen many generations of men grow up, do good or evil deeds, and die, sometimes leaving grand monuments upon the earth, sometimes disappearing from knowledge like the very birds, leaving scarcely a trace behind.

In his time great kings had lived and reigned and turned to dust. Prophets had grown hoary, said their word, and passed away, leaving no echo. Poets had sung and had died singing. But the Phoenix, looking down from the palms of his desert, saw it all and did not die.

All this had been his pride and honor. How he had enjoyed his strength, his beauty, his wisdom, and the knowledge that he was honored and adored by thousands who had never even seen his glory! But now, now all was changed. He was grown old and tired. He felt his loneliness and he longed to die.

His wings were feeble. Of late he had not dared to venture far from the desert. He dreaded the curious gaze of the other birds, who would find his beauty dimmed, and would scorn, perchance, the faded glory which they had once held in awe. For years he had not ventured within sight of men, and he knew that most of them had forgotten his existence, nay, even denied that he had ever lived. He feared that there might not be a single heart in all the world that thrilled to his name.

Thinking thus mournfully, the Phoenix sat upon the top of the tallest palm. His plumage of crimson and gold glowed in the last rays of the setting sun. His head was drooping, and his eye lustreless. The joy of life was gone. Slowly the Sun sank towards the horizon, a red eye fixed upon the Phoenix steadily. Suddenly across the gray waste of sand dotted a beam of light, intensely bright. A single ray from that watchful Eye seemed to flame as it reached the palm tree and pierced to the very heart of the Phoenix. A thrill ran through his body. He drew himself together, and his eye gleamed with new lustre as he fixed it steadily upon the dazzling disk just touching the horizon. Dark stood the palm against the desert, but the Phoenix was bathed in sudden light. It was the signal, the signal for which he had been waiting, though he knew it not. The five hundred years were ended. The mystery of his life was about to be solved.

As the sun sank below the horizon, eagerly the Phoenix set about the task which was before him. At last he might build the nest which till now he had never known. On the top of the highest palm he would build it, that it might receive from the blessed East the first beam of the morning sun. Marvelously strengthened for the task, back and forth to the ends of the earth his wings of crimson and gold bore the Phoenix that night. For this was to be no nest of sticks and straw. Of precious things must it be made, and well he knew where such were to be found. Of silky leaves and grass interwoven with splinters of sandal-wood were the walls. Then on the bottom of the nest he laid, bit by bit, a pile of sweet-smelling gums, cinnamon and spice, spikenard, myrrh, camphor, ambergris, and frankincense, with no meaner choice.

All night he labored, beak and talon, until the nest was ready. And as the first tints of dawn began to streak the east, the Phoenix rose once, high into the air, gazing with wistful eyes over the world which he had loved; then, slowly sinking to the palm, he poised his gorgeous body upon the fragrant nest. With wings spread wide, and eyes fixed eagerly upon the spot where the Sun was sure to rise, he waited, waited.

At last the golden Eye appeared. As on the night before, one radiant beam seemed to single out the lonely palm. One shaft of flame pierced to the nest whereon the Phoenix sat. It was the final signal to the Bird of the Sun. Immediately the great bird began to fan the sweet-smelling mass with his wings. The burning ray grew brighter,--a pungent, wonderful aroma of mingled fragrances filled the air. Gradually the Sun rose, great and glorious, and as it advanced into the heaven a thin cloud of smoke floated from the palm tree, and wound away across the desert towards the east. Faster and faster fanned the great wings of the Phoenix, until when the Sun shone full down through the palm tree top, the whole mass burst into flame, in the midst of which the Phoenix blended crimson and gold. High in the air rose the fire, diffusing abroad all the sweet odors of Araby the blest. For a little while it glowed, then gradually sank, lower and lower, until but a pile of ashes remained at the bottom of the nest.

But lo! Was the Phoenix dead? What was this creature risen in youth and beauty from the ashes? A bird like the Eagle in shape, but nobler, larger, stronger, more gracious even than the King of Birds, a brilliant vision of crimson and gold, rose like a flame from the nest, hung for a moment above the palm, looking eagerly at the Sun, which baptized him in its splendor. A new Phoenix lived in the world. Once more the ancient glory was renewed. Once more youth, joy, and hope sprang from the Phoenix's ashes and rejoiced in the centuries of sunshine before him. Death was indeed worth dying to make this life worth living!

Slowly the young Phoenix descended to the nest which had been at once a sepulchre and a cradle. Tenderly careful of the parent ashes which it held, with lusty beak and talon he tore the nest bodily from the branches, and set out upon his pious journey. He knew not where he went, nor why, but the Sun drew him to the East.

As he sped, through the sky, a flash of gold and crimson, the lesser birds gathered to wonder and admire. Flocks of them followed at a distance, a train of worshipers, chorusing the glory of the new-born wonder. He bore his head high with its burden, and his heart was filled with pious joy. It was good to be a Phoenix, good, good!

At last he reached the place which unknowingly he sought. The Sun alone had been his guide. To the city of Heliopolis in Egypt he came; to the great Temple of the Sun, brightly adorned with crimson and gold, the Phoenix colors.

There upon the altar he laid the precious ashes. And lo! There were folk waiting to receive them,--many little children, and some elders of childlike heart, who took the ashes and laid them reverently in the shrine. The Phoenix was not forgotten; he was never to be forgotten so long as the world should last.

The new Phoenix flew back to the Arabian desert to live his five hundred years as each of his race had done, sacred, afar, and apart, but not forgotten, though in his old age he might come to deem so. For in the bright Temple of the Sun there are always folk of childlike sympathy who delight to honor the eternal Phoenix of romance and mystery,--the dear, undying memory of a time long past.

THE END